Practical Machine Learning in JavaScript

TensorFlow.js for
Web Developers

Charlie Gerard

Apress®

Practical Machine Learning in JavaScript: TensorFlow.js for Web Developers

Charlie Gerard
Les Clayes sous bois, France

ISBN-13 (pbk): 978-1-4842-6417-1   ISBN-13 (electronic): 978-1-4842-6418-8
https://doi.org/10.1007/978-1-4842-6418-8

Copyright © 2021 by Charlie Gerard

Managing Director, Apress Media LLC: Welmoed Spahr
Acquisitions Editor: Aaron Black
Development Editor: James Markham
Coordinating Editor: Jessica Vakili

Distributed to the book trade worldwide by Springer Science+Business Media New York, 1 NY Plazar, New York, NY 10014. Phone 1-800-SPRINGER, fax (201) 348-4505, e-mail orders-ny@springer-sbm.com, or visit www.springeronline.com. Apress Media, LLC is a California LLC and the sole member (owner) is Springer Science + Business Media Finance Inc (SSBM Finance Inc). SSBM Finance Inc is a **Delaware** corporation.

For information on translations, please e-mail booktranslations@springernature.com; for reprint, paperback, or audio rights, please e-mail bookpermissions@springernature.com.

Apress titles may be purchased in bulk for academic, corporate, or promotional use. eBook versions and licenses are also available for most titles. For more information, reference our Print and eBook Bulk Sales web page at http://www.apress.com/bulk-sales.

Any source code or other supplementary material referenced by the author in this book is available to readers on GitHub via the book's product page, located at www.apress.com/978-1-4842-6417-1. For more detailed information, please visit http://www.apress.com/source-code.

Printed on acid-free paper

*To Joel, Jack and Daisy, just because. To me, for pushing
through a very tough year and still doing my
best writing this book.*

Table of Contents

About the Author ix

About the Technical Reviewer xi

Acknowledgments xiii

Introduction xv

Chapter 1: The basics of machine learning 1

1.1 What is machine learning?..1

1.2 Types of machine learning 8

　1.2.1 Supervised learning 9

　1.2.2 Unsupervised learning...10

　1.2.3 Reinforcement learning 12

　1.2.4 Semi-supervised learning 13

1.3 Algorithms..14

　1.3.1 Naive Bayes...14

　1.3.2 K-nearest neighbors 15

　1.3.3 Convolutional neural networks 16

1.4 Applications..18

　1.4.1 Healthcare 18

　1.4.2 Home automation 20

　1.4.3 Social good 21

　1.4.4 Art 23

1.5 Summary...24

Chapter 2: TensorFlow.js 25

2.1 Basics of TensorFlow.js... 25

    2.1.1 Creating tensors 26

    2.1.2 Accessing data in tensors 30

    2.1.3 Operations on tensors 31

    2.1.4 Memory 33

2.2 Features 34

    2.2.1 Using a pre-trained model.. 34

    2.2.2 Transfer learning... 38

    2.2.3 Creating, training, and predicting 41

Chapter 3: Building an image classifier 45

3.1 Using a pre-trained model 45

3.2 Transfer learning.. 55

Chapter 4: Text classification and sentiment analysis 67

4.1 What is sentiment analysis? 67

4.2 How does natural language processing work?........................... 68

    4.2.1 Common concepts – Basics of NLP................................. 68

4.3 Implementing sentiment analysis in TensorFlow.js................... 74

    4.3.1 Positive, negative, and neutral....................................... 74

    4.3.2 Toxicity Classifier 84

4.4 Applications... 91

    4.4.1 Cognitive assistants and computer therapy 91

    4.4.2 Social media monitoring.. 95

    4.4.3 Automation tools.. 98

4.5 Other types of text classification tools 99

    4.5.1 Intent analysis 99

    4.5.2 Named Entity Recognition 100

    4.5.3 Text summarization 101

    4.5.4 Question Answering with TensorFlow.js 102

Chapter 5: Experimenting with inputs 135

5.1 Audio data 135

    5.1.1 What is sound? 137

    5.1.2 Accessing audio data.. 138

    5.1.3 Visualizing audio data... 143

    5.1.4 Training the classifier 152

    5.1.5 Predictions.. 157

    5.1.6 Transfer learning API 164

    5.1.7 Applications 169

    5.1.8 Limits.. 174

5.2 Body and movement tracking 182

    5.2.1 Facemesh 183

    5.2.2 Handpose.. 199

    5.2.3 PoseNet 219

5.3 Hardware data 245

    5.3.1 Web Sensors API... 247

    5.3.2 Accessing sensors data... 248

    5.3.3 Setting up web sockets 251

    5.3.4 Data processing... 259

    5.3.5 Creating and training the model 274

    5.3.6 Live predictions 282

Chapter 6: Machine learning in production 287

6.1 Challenges 287

    6.1.1 Scalability 288

    6.1.2 High availability 288

    6.1.3 Observability...288

    6.1.4 Reusability...289

6.2 Machine learning life cycle 289

6.3 Machine learning systems 292

6.4 Tools 300

    6.4.1 Pre-trained models..300

    6.4.2 APIs...300

    6.4.3 Serving platforms 301

Chapter 7: Bias in machine learning 305

7.1 What is bias?..305

7.2 Examples of bias in machine learning 307

    7.2.1 Gender bias 307

    7.2.2 Racial bias 308

7.3 Potential solutions 310

    7.3.1 Framing the problem 310

    7.3.2 Collecting the data..311

    7.3.3 Data preparation...313

    7.3.4 Team diversity 314

7.4 Challenges 314

Index...317

About the Author

Charlie Gerard is a senior front-end developer at Netlify, a Google Developer Expert in Web Technologies, and a Mozilla Tech Speaker. She is passionate about exploring the possibilities of the Web and spends her personal time building interactive prototypes using hardware, creative coding, and machine learning. She has been diving into ML in JavaScript for over a year and built a variety of projects. She's excited to share what she's learned and help more developers get started.

About the Technical Reviewer

David Pazmino has been developing software applications for 20 years in Fortune 100 companies. He is an experienced developer in front-end and back-end development who specializes in developing machine learning models for financial applications. David has developed many applications in Node.js, Angular.js, and React.js. He currently develops applications in Scala and Python for deep learning neural networks using TensorFlow 2.0. David has a degree from Cornell University, a master's from Pace University in Computer Science, and a master's from Northwestern in Predictive Analytics.

Acknowledgments

First of all, thanks to everyone involved in the creation of this book, including my publisher, my editor and my technical reviewers, for giving me this opportunity. Additionally, thanks to the TensorFlow.js team for creating the framework this book relies on. Their work and dedication to make machine learning more accessible to web developers has been essential to my research and work over the past couple of years. Finally, special thanks to my close friends for their constant support throughout the years and to the community of people who have been following my work and sharing my passion for creating useless (but not worthless) projects. This would not have been possible without you and I am forever grateful.

Introduction

Even though machine learning (ML) isn't a new technology, improvements in techniques and algorithms over the past few years have brought it to the forefront of technology, making it possibly one of the most exciting and promising tool to solve complex problems.

In general, most production machine learning applications are developed using programming languages such as Python or R, by researchers, machine learning engineers and data scientist; however, in recent years, new tools have been built in the aim to make machine learning more accessible to a wider range of developers.

In this book, we will focus on TensorFlow.js, a multi-features JavaScript library developed by Google that empowers web developers to build ML-enabled applications in the browser or in Node.js.

You might be thinking: "Why would I read a book about machine learning in JavaScript if most ML-enabled applications use Python or R in production?", or, "Why would I learn about machine learning if I am a web developer?". These questions are valid, especially considering that machine learning is a very different discipline than web development. However, in the technology field, a part of our work is to keep up to date with what is going on, not necessarily becoming an expert at every new technology or tool, but at least have an idea of the possibilities and limits. In my opinion, this is why tools like TensorFlow.js are important. Having the possibility to explore a new topic without having to also learn another programming language breaks down the barrier considerably. Besides, considering how fast things are moving and how powerful these tools are 13 becoming, we can imagine a future where "JavaScript machine learning engineer" would be a sought-after job title. After all, I would have never imagined "Futurist" would be one.

All this to say that the aim of this book is to introduce machine learning in a more approachable way, to break down barriers and hopefully make you feel more comfortable with this technology. After reading, you should have a good understanding of the current features offered by machine learning frameworks in JavaScript. To do this, we'll define some of the commonly used terms and concepts you will open come across, we'll cover the basics of ML using TensorFlow.js, and we'll build a variety of projects to understand what is currently possible as well as some of the pitfalls. By the end, you should be able to, not only understand the theory, but also build machine learning enabled web applications.

An important thing to note however, is that this book is not going to look into how different machine learning algorithms are being developed. We're not going to dive into their source code, but instead, learn to identify their use cases and how to implement them. This book is aimed at being an introduction for people who want to learn more about machine learning in a practical way, without getting too deep into advanced topics.

Finally, and more importantly, I wanted to make this book as engaging as possible, so the different projects you will build involve various inputs such as images, the video from your webcam feed, the audio from your computer's microphone, text data you can replace, and even motion data!

Machine learning can be fun so, if this sounds interesting to you, I hope you'll like this book.

CHAPTER 1

The basics of machine learning

1.1 What is machine learning?

Over the past few years, you've probably heard the words "machine learning" many times, but what is it exactly? Is it the same thing as artificial intelligence? What about deep learning? Neural networks? Models?

Before diving deeper into the tools, algorithms, and what can be built, let's start by defining some of these terms to gain a common understanding of what machine learning is and is not.

Artificial intelligence, machine learning, and deep learning are all related terms. However, they're not exactly the same thing, they're more like subsets of each other.

© Charlie Gerard 2021
C. Gerard, *Practical Machine Learning in JavaScript*,
https://doi.org/10.1007/978-1-4842-6418-8_1

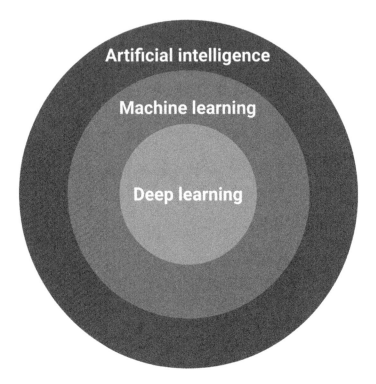

Figure 1-1. *This graph is a representation of how artificial intelligence, machine learning, and deep learning connect*

Artificial intelligence is the umbrella term for everything related to the expression of "intelligence" by computers. This can include speech recognition (the understanding of human speech), autonomous cars, or strategic gaming (the ability for computers to play strategic games like Go or Chess).

Machine learning represents the technology itself: all the practices and set of tools to give the ability to computers to find patterns in data without being explicitly programmed.

This includes the different types of learning and algorithms available such as supervised learning, Naive Bayes, K-nearest neighbors, and so on that we will cover in the next few chapters.

This technology is used to train computers to make their own predictions based on a developed understanding of historical data.

What this means is that we're not telling computers exactly what to look for; instead, we feed algorithms a lot of data previously collected and let them find patterns and correlations in this dataset to draw future conclusions and probabilities when given new data.

For example, if we want to use machine learning to help us calculate the probability of a person having cancer based on their CT scans, we would build a dataset of hundreds of thousands, or even millions, of CT scans from diverse patients around the world. We would label this data between CT scans of cancerous patients and scans of healthy patients. We would then feed all this data to machine learning algorithms and let them find patterns in those medical images to try and develop an accurate understanding of what a cancerous scan looks like.

Then, using the model generated by all this training, we would be able to use it on a new scan that wasn't part of the training data, and generate a probability of a patient having cancer or not.

Finally, **deep learning** is a specific tool or method. It is related to another term you might be familiar with, called **artificial neural networks**. Deep learning is the subset of machine learning that uses algorithms inspired by the structure and function of the brain.

The concept of neural networks in machine learning is not new, but the term deep learning is more recent.

Essentially, this method allows the training of large neural networks in the aim to make revolutionary advances in machine learning and AI.

Deep learning has been taking off over the past few years mainly thanks to advancements in computing power and the amount of data we are now collecting.

In comparison to other machine learning algorithms, deep learning ones have a performance that continues to improve as we increase the amount of data we feed them, which makes them more scalable where others plateau.

A representation of this can be found in this slide from a talk by Andrew Ng at ExtractConf 2015 entitled "What data scientists should know about deep learning."

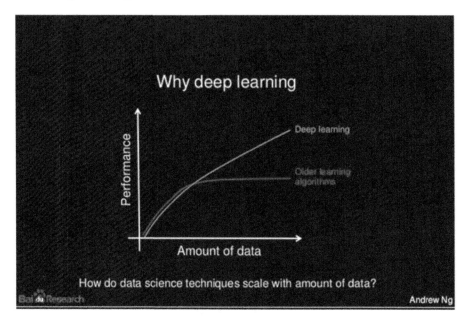

Figure 1-2. *This slide illustrates how deep learning scales compared to other machine learning algorithms. Source:* `https://www.slideshare.net/ExtractConf`

As you can see in the preceding graph, the main differential characteristic of deep learning algorithms is their ability to scale and increase performance with more data.

The term "deep" learning generally refers to the amount of layers used in the neural networks. If this does not totally make sense right now, we'll cover the concept of layers a bit later in this book.

Now that we know more about the difference between these terms, this book is going to be focusing mainly on machine learning, the technology.

We'll be diving a little bit into deep learning as we look into different techniques but we'll touch on broader aspects of the technology as well.

We've defined the different names sometimes interchangeably used to talk about intelligence expressed by computers, but what about other important idioms like "neural networks," "algorithms," and "models"?

We are probably going to mention them along the book, so let's spend the next few paragraphs defining them.

Let's start with **algorithms** as this is the one you might be the most familiar with as it is already used in traditional programming.

An algorithm can be defined as a set of rules or instructions to solve a particular problem or perform a computation.

In software engineering, examples of algorithms you might have heard of or used would be the quicksort algorithm, the Dijkstra algorithm, binary search, and so on. Each algorithm was created to solve a particular problem.

When it comes to machine learning algorithms, they solve different types of problems but the concept is the same; each algorithm, it being a support vector machine (SVM) or a long short-term memory (LSTM) algorithm, is only a mathematical function that solves a specific problem.

Neural networks are a set of deep learning algorithms designed to mimic the way the brain works.

The same way the brain is made of a giant network of connected neurons, neural networks are made of layers of interconnected nodes called artificial neurons.

A visual way of representing these networks might be like the following graph.

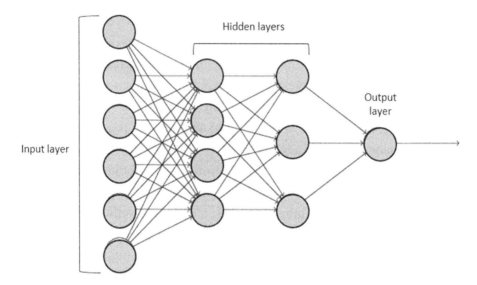

Figure 1-3. *This graph is a representation of the different layers in a neural network*

In neural networks, there are usually three main parts, an **input layer** that represents the input data you want to generate a prediction for (e.g., an image you want to apply object detection to, a piece of text you want to get the sentiment for, etc.), a certain number of **hidden layers**, and an **output layer** that represents your prediction.

This is a very high-level explanation of how neural networks work, but the most important part to understand is that they are made of a large number of interconnected nodes, organized in layers, that get activated or not during the training process depending on the outcome generated by neurons in the previous layer, in a similar way different neurons in the brain fire when given specific inputs.

Finally, **models**. In machine learning, models represent the output of a training session. When the training process is happening, algorithms are "learning" to draw conclusions from patterns they find in data; once the training steps are done, the output is a model.

Models are mathematical functions that can take new inputs as parameters and produce a prediction as output.

For example, image classification models have been trained with thousands of labelled images to recognize patterns in the data and predict the presence of certain entities (e.g., cats, dogs, cars, people, etc.). When using an image classification model in a new application, you would be able to feed it a new image that might not have been part of the training dataset, and have it generate a prediction of what might be in this image it has never "seen" before based on the learnings from the training process.

At the end of the training process, you generally test your model with new input that was not part of the training dataset to test the validity of the prediction generated.

Now that we've defined a few of the important terms you'll come across when diving into machine learning, I think it is important to go quickly over what machine learning **is not**.

Hopefully, the last few paragraphs made it more clear that machine learning is not able to generate predictions without being fed some pregathered data.

The same way we, as humans, cannot recognize a new object or entity we've never been exposed to, an algorithm also needs to be given some kind of information before being able to identify a new input.

For example, the first time I heard about 3D printers, I was struggling to be able to visualize what it was. When I finally saw and interacted with one, I then had an understanding of what the object was and was able to recognize future ones.

The brain does this very fast, but algorithms need a lot more data to be trained with before being able to develop an understanding of what objects are.

Because algorithms are basically mathematical functions, it is important to take with a grain of salt what you can read about the evolution of AI in the future.

As performant as it can be, AI systems still need to be trained on a lot of data we have to previously gather. As a result, I believe the opportunity of machine learning applications resides in **augmenting** humans rather than **replacing** them.

An example of that would be in the field of healthcare. I don't particularly believe that AI systems will replace doctors, but we're already seeing how machine learning helps them by being able to process a massive amount of medical images and identify and diagnose diseases in CT scans and MRIs, sometimes with higher accuracy than healthcare professionals.

By relying on machine learning models this way, we can hope to diagnose and help people faster.

It is also important to remember that computers don't have a real understanding of the context of the information they are working with. Certain problems we need to solve are very complex from a societal point of view and should probably not be solved using machine learning only. We will cover a bit more about the topic of ethics and AI toward the end of this book.

1.2 Types of machine learning

Problems solved using machine learning usually fall into one of the three main categories: supervised learning, unsupervised learning, and reinforcement learning.

You might also hear about semi-supervised learning, but this book is not going to cover it.

Knowing which type of problem you are trying to solve is important because it will determine which algorithms you'll want to use, how you will prepare your data, and what kind of output you will get.

First of all, let's start with the most popular one, **supervised learning**.

1.2.1 Supervised learning

Supervised learning is the ability to find patterns in data using both
features and **labels**.

Here, we just introduced two new data-related terms we need to define
before we keep going.

When using a dataset, **features** represent the characteristics of each
entry and **labels** are how you would define these entries. Let's use an
example to put this in practice.

Let's say you want to sell your house but are not sure about what price
would be the most competitive on the market, but you have access to a
large dataset containing information about all the houses and their price,
in the city you live in.

In this case, the **features** would be details about each house (number
of bedrooms, bathrooms, floors, type of house, does it have a balcony,
garden, etc.), and the **labels** would be their price.

It could look something like this.

Table 1-1. *This table represents an example of a labelled dataset*

Price	Number of bedrooms	Number of bathrooms	Number of floors	Balcony	Garden
$1,500,000	3	2	2	No	Yes
$500,000	1	1	1	Yes	No
$750,000	1	1	1	No	Yes
$1,700,000	4	2	2	No	Yes
$700,000	2	1	1	No	No
$850,000	2	1	1	Yes	Yes
$525,000	1	1	1	No	No
$2,125,000	5	3	3	Yes	Yes
$645,000	1	1	1	Yes	Yes

A real dataset would have many more entries and more features would be gathered, but this is only an example to illustrate the concept of features and labels.

Using this labelled data, we can use machine learning to predict the price at which your house should be put on the market for.

For example, based on the preceding data, if your house had 1 bedroom, 1 bathroom, no balcony but a garden, its price would be closer to about $750,000 than $1,000,000.

In this quick example, we can do it manually by looking at the data, but in a real-life situation, the amount of data would be much larger, and using machine learning would be able to do this calculation much faster than humans.

Some other examples of supervised learning problems include predicting if an email is spam or not, predicting the probability of a sports team winning based on previous game data, predicting the probability of an insurance claim being fraudulent.

In summary, supervised learning is the creation of predictions based on **labelled data**.

1.2.2 Unsupervised learning

Another common type of learning is called **unsupervised learning**. Contrary to supervised learning, unsupervised learning is the creation of predictions based on **unlabelled data**. What this means is that we rely **only on the set of features**.

If we think about our previous dataset of houses, it means we would remove the column "Price" and would end up only with the data about the characteristics of each house.

If we reuse the scenario of wanting to predict the price at which we should sell our house, you might be wondering, how can we predict this price if our data is not labelled (does not contain any price)?

This is where the importance of thinking about the problem you are trying to solve and paying attention to the data you possess comes into play.

With unsupervised learning, we are not trying to predict a single outcome, or answer a specific question, but instead, identify trends.

In our house problem, our question was "How much can I sell my house for?" where we would expect a specific price as an outcome. However, as mentioned previously in this book, a machine learning algorithm cannot really predict a price if the dataset it was fed with during training did not contain any price.

Therefore, this is not the type of situation where we would use unsupervised learning.

As unsupervised learning is about identifying trends and classifying data into groups, a good example of problems that would fall into this space would be **predicting customer behavior**.

With this type of problem, we are not trying to answer a question with a specific answer; instead, we are trying to classify data into different categories so we can create clusters of entities with similar features.

Using our example of predicting customer behavior, by gathering data about each customer, we can use machine learning to find behavioral correlation between customers and find buying patterns that would help in applications such as advertising.

Gathering and using data about where you shop, at what time, how many times a week, what you buy, and so on, we can draw conclusions about your gender, age, socioeconomic background, and more, which can then be used to predict what you might be likely to buy based on the cluster you belong to.

You might be familiar with a real-world application of this type of prediction if you've been exposed to music recommendation on Spotify or product recommendation on Amazon.

Based on your listening and buying habits, companies gather data and use machine learning to cluster customers into groups, and based on what other people like you have listened to, they propose recommendations of songs or products you might like.

1.2.3 Reinforcement learning

A third type of learning is called **reinforcement learning**. If you're reading this book, you are likely just getting started with machine learning so you probably won't be using it at first.

Reinforcement learning is mostly used for applications such as self-driving cars, games with AI players, and so on where the outcome involves more of a behavior or set of actions.

It relies on the concept of reward and penalty and the relationship between an "agent" and an "environment."

We can imagine the scenario of a game of Pong where the environment is the game and the agent is a player. Actions from the player change the state of the game. Changing the position of the paddles influences where the ball goes and eventually results in the player winning or losing.

When a sequence of actions results in the player winning, the system gets some kind of reward to indicate that this particular set of interactions resulted in achieving the goal of the training process, creating an AI player that can win a game by itself.

The training process then continues, iterating over different sets of interactions, getting rewards when winning (+1 point), a penalty when losing (-1 point), and correcting itself to develop an understanding of how to win the game against another player over time.

This type of learning does not rely on a preexisting dataset used to feed an algorithm.

Instead, it uses a set of goals and rules (e.g., the paddle can only go up and down, the goal is to win against the other player, etc.) to learn by itself the correct behavior to optimize its opportunities to achieve the set goal.

Reinforcement learning lets the system explore an environment and make its own decisions.

This type of learning often demands a very long training process involving a huge amount of steps. One of the issues resides in the fact that, when receiving a penalty for losing a game, the system assumes that the entire sequence of actions taken in the round caused it to lose. As a result, it will avoid taking all these steps again instead of identifying which steps in the action sequence contributed to losing.

1.2.4 Semi-supervised learning

Finally, let's talk briefly about semi-supervised learning.

Semi-supervised learning sits between supervised and unsupervised learning. As mentioned in the last few pages, supervised learning deals with labelled data and unsupervised learning uses unlabelled data.

Sometimes, when using a large dataset of unlabelled data, we can proceed to label a subset of it and use semi-supervised learning to do what is called **pseudo-labelling**.

What this means is that we're going to manually label a portion of our dataset and let the algorithm label the rest to end up with a fully labelled set.

For example, if we have a collection of hundreds of thousands of images of cats and dogs that are not already labelled, we can label a part of it ourselves and feed it to a semi-supervised learning algorithm that is going to find patterns in these images and is going to be able to take the rest of the unlabelled dataset as input and attach the label "cat" or "dog" to each new image, resulting in all the data being labelled.

This technique allows us to generate a labelled dataset much faster than having to do it manually so we can then proceed to use supervised learning on it.

Understanding which type of learning your problem falls into is usually one of the first steps.

Now that we've covered the main ones, let's look into some of the most well-known algorithms.

1.3 Algorithms

As with standard programming, machine learning uses algorithms to help solve problems.

However, it is not essential to understand the implementation of all algorithms before being able to use them. The most important is to learn which type of learning they belong to and the type of data they are the most efficient with.

If you compare it with web programming, there are a lot of different JavaScript frameworks available, and you don't necessarily need to understand their source code to be able to build your applications using them. What you need to know, however, is if they support the features you need.

In the context of machine learning, some algorithms are very good at working with image data, while others are better at handling text data.

Let's dive into some of them.

1.3.1 Naive Bayes

The Naive Bayes algorithm is a supervised learning classification algorithm.

It predicts the probability of different classes based on various attributes and prior knowledge.

It is mostly used in text classification and with problems having multiple classes. It is considered highly scalable and requires less training data than other algorithms.

A practical example of problem that could be solved with Naive Bayes would be around filming a TV series.

Unless all of the plot happens indoors, the production of the show will be impacted by environmental factors such as the weather, humidity level, temperature, wind, season, and so on.

As parts of a TV show are not filmed in order, we could use machine learning to help us find the best days certain parts of the show should be filmed on, based on the requirements of certain scenes.

Gathering a dataset of weather attributes and whether or not an outdoor scene was filmed, we would be able to predict the probability of being able to film a new scene on a future day.

This algorithm is called "Naive" as it makes the assumption that all the variables in the dataset are not correlated to each other.

For example, a rainy day does not have to also be windy or a high level of humidity does not have to correlate to a high temperature.

1.3.2 K-nearest neighbors

Another popular algorithm is called **K-nearest neighbors**.

This algorithm is a classification algorithm that assumes that similar things exist in close proximity to each other, so near each other.

A good way to illustrate this is with an example graph. When working on machine learning problems, you can visualize data like this.

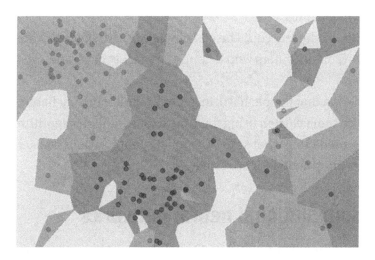

Figure 1-4. *This illustration represents a visualization generated by using a K-nearest neighbors classification algorithm. Source:* `https://machinelearningmastery.com/tutorial-to-implement-k-nearest-neighbors-in-python-from-scratch/`

In the preceding visualization, we can see that the data plotted ends up creating some kind of organized clusters. Similar data points exist close to each other.

The K-nearest neighbors algorithm (KNN) works on this idea of similarity to classify new data.

When using this algorithm, we need to define a value for "K" that will represent the amount of closest data points (neighbors) we will take into consideration to help us classify a new entry.

For example, if we pick the value K = 10, when we want to predict the class for a new entry, we look at the 10 closest neighbors and their class. The class that has the highest amount of neighbors to our new data point is the class that is predicted to be the correct one.

A practical example for this would be in predicting customer behavior or likelihood to buy certain items.

A supermarket chain has access to data from people's purchases and could use unsupervised learning to organize customers into clusters based on their buying habits.

Examples of clusters could be customers who are single vs. those who have a family, or customers who belong to a bracket of certain ages (young vs. old).

Considering that people have, in general, similar buying habits to people in the same cluster, using the K-nearest neighbors algorithm would be useful in predicting what kind of products people would be likely to buy and use this information for advertising.

1.3.3 Convolutional neural networks

Convolutional neural network, also known as ConvNet or CNN, is an algorithm that performs really well at classifying images. It can be used for problems such as object detection and face recognition.

Unlike humans, computers process images as an array of pixels which length would be equal to height * width * dimension. A RGB image of 16x16 pixels would be interpreted as a matrix of 16*16*3 so an array of 768 values.

A classic example of problem solved using a CNN is using the MNIST dataset of handwritten digits.

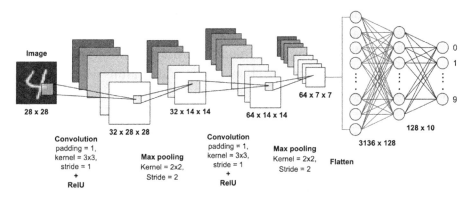

Figure 1-5. *This is a representation of how a convolutional network works, from an input image to hidden layers, and outputting a number Source:* https://towardsdatascience.com/mnist-handwritten-digits-classification-using-a-convolutional-neural-network-cnn-af5fafbc35e9

The preceding image illustrates how a convolutional neural network would predict the number handwritten in the input image.

It would start by transforming the image into an array of 2352 values (28*28*3) to transform a 3D input into a 1D one. It would then run the data into different layers and filters of the neural network to end up with an output layer of 10 options, as the digit to predict would be between 0 and 9.

The output of the prediction would be a probability for each entry of the output layer, and the entry with the highest probability would be the correct one.

If the problem you are trying to solve involves a dataset of images, you probably want to play around with a CNN algorithm.

These three algorithms fall into different categories. Naive Bayes belongs to Bayesian algorithms, K-nearest neighbors to instance-based algorithms, and convolutional neural networks (CNN) to deep learning algorithms.

There are a lot more categories and algorithms to explore; however, covering all of them is not the goal of this book. As you dive deeper into machine learning and build your own applications, you should definitely look into more of them as you experiment. There is not always a single solution to a problem, so learning about different algorithms will allow you to find the one best suited to what you are trying to achieve.

1.4 Applications

Some applications were mentioned in the last few pages of this book when attempting to illustrate concepts with examples; however, there are many more use cases for machine learning in various fields.

1.4.1 Healthcare

An example of using machine learning in healthcare was introduced when I talked about how systems can be used to detect diseases in CT scans.

Apart from making diagnoses from image analysis, other applications in this field include treatment personalization and "data wrangling" of personal records.

Clinical data is not always digital, with a lot of forms and prescriptions still being handwritten; and if it is digital, each health system customizes their Electronic Health Records (EHR), making the data collected in one hospital different from the data collected at others.

Data wrangling is the concept of capturing, organizing, and triaging data. Using Optical Character Recognition (OCR), a system could scan a handwritten document, parse words, and use a technique called "entity extraction" to understand them and their semantical relationship to each other.

This way, medical documents can be automatically saved in a database, respecting the same format, which makes it easier to search, analyze, or use in the future.

A few of the biggest tech companies dedicate a part of their research center to the development of innovative solutions in this space.

Microsoft, for example, is working on a few research projects like project InnerEye, that aims to turn radiological images into measuring devices. Using machine learning algorithms, the goal of this project is to automatically detect tumors in 3D radiological images, as well as generating precise surgery planning and navigation.

IBM has a project called IBM Watson for Oncology that helps physicians identify key information in a patient's medical record to help explore personalized treatment options.

Google has developed a protocol buffer for the Fast Healthcare Interoperability Resources (FHIR) standard that aims at homogenizing the way medical data is stored, so developers can build machine learning systems that can be used by any healthcare institution.

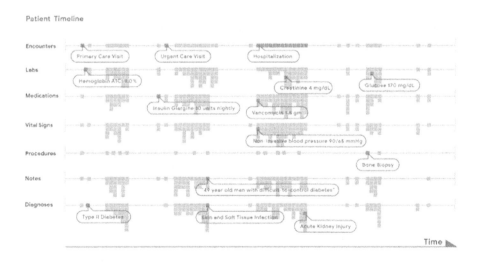

Figure 1-6. *Example of timeline built using patient's health records. Source: https://ai.googleblog.com/2018/05/deep-learning-for-electronic-health.html*

The preceding visualization represents a timeline of patient's health record data. Each gray dot is a piece of data stored in the open data standard FHIR. A deep learning model can then analyze this data to make predictions.

1.4.2 Home automation

The application for machine learning you might be the most familiar with is in home automation.

You probably have heard of, or may even possess, some Internet of Things devices that use machine learning such as the Amazon Alexa or Google Home.

These devices use speech recognition algorithms and natural language processing (NLP) to identify the words you are saying, analyze the intent, and provide the most accurate response possible.

Something worth mentioning is that there is a difference between a "connected" device and a "smart" one. The Internet of Things can be defined as a network of connected "things," meaning that devices are connected to each other, usually via Wi-Fi or Bluetooth.

However, some devices are simply connected, such as the Philips Hue light bulb, that you can control remotely from your phone. It does not use any machine learning algorithm to produce any output; it only turns on and off or changes color.

On the other hand, devices like the Nest thermostat would fall into the category of "smart devices." It implements a more complex functionality as it really learns from your behavior over time. As you change the temperature of your house over a period of time, sometimes even during the same day, it learns your habits and adapts automatically.

Just like the Philips Hue, it also lets you control it from anywhere using your phone, but the additional learning part is an example of using machine learning in home automation.

Some research centers are working on improving devices like the Google Home to go beyond speech recognition toward activity recognition.

Leveraging the device's microphone, you can use machine learning algorithms and sound data to predict what a user is currently doing or which room they are in. Accessing this information would allow us to build more personalized smart systems. You could imagine listening to a recipe using a Google Home, following step by step, and the device would be able to pause automatically when it recognizes that you are chopping something, or using a whisk, and so on based on recognizing patterns in the sound data it is receiving.

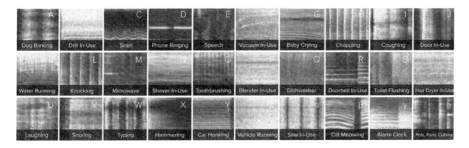

Figure 1-7. *Examples of spectrograms representing the sound data produced by different activities. Source:* `www.gierad.com/projects/ubicoustics/`

1.4.3 Social good

There is a rising fear in the consequences of using machine learning to solve certain problems, for example, in the justice system; however, there is also a lot of potential of using it for social good.

Either it be for animal protection or to prevent deforestation, the applications of machine learning in this space are very exciting.

Some projects aim to protect endangered species like the killer whales (also known as orcas) in the Salish Sea, from British Columbia to

Washington State. With only about 73 of them left, Google partnered with Fisheries and Oceans Canada (DFO), as well as Rainforest Connection, to track and monitor orca's behavior using deep neural networks.

Teaching a machine learning model to recognize orca sounds, it can then detect the presence of the animal and alert experts in real time. This type of system can help monitor the animals' health and protect them in the event of an oil spill, for example.

Another project by Rainforest Connection aims to prevent illegal deforestation using machine learning and used cell phones.

The devices monitor the sounds of the forest, 24 hours a day, send all the audio data to the cloud, and, using TensorFlow, analyze it in real time to identify chainsaws, logging trucks, and all sounds of illegal activity to alert locals.

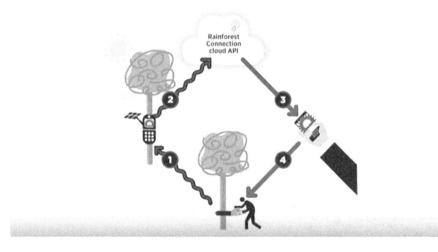

Figure 1-8. *Visual representation of how the Rainforest Connection project against illegal deforestation works. Source:* www.ted.com/ talks/topher_white_what_can_save_the_rainforest_your_used_ cell_phone#t-289131

There are plenty more interesting projects focusing on leveraging the possibilities of machine learning to help social causes. Even though this is not the focus of this book, I encourage you to do further research if this is something you would like to contribute to.

1.4.4 Art

Art might not be your first concern when wanting to learn more about machine learning; however, I really think its importance is deeply underrated in the field of technology.

Art very often experiments with the latest technological innovations much faster than any other field.

Monitoring how machine learning is used in creative ways can give us an idea of how far the technology can go.

Not only is it important to expose yourself to the work of artists, but I would also recommend trying to build creative applications yourself.

Spending some time working on a creative way to implement a certain technology to your project will give you the opportunity to explore parts of the tool you might have never thought of before.

Creativity can help you identify new use cases, opportunities, and limits of the tools you are using.

Especially in a field like machine learning, where so many things are still unknown, there is a vast potential to come up with new ideas of what is possible.

Some examples of machine learning used in creative ways are in the work of artists like Memo Akten. In his project "Learning to See," he uses deep neural networks and a live camera input to try to make sense of what it sees, in the context of what it has seen before.

Figure 1-9. *Sample from art project "Learning to See" by Memo Akten. Source:* `www.memo.tv/portfolio/gloomy-sunday/`

A model has been trained with images of oceans. It is given a new input from a camera feed (on the left), analyses it, and tries to understand its meaning based on the training data it was fed with. The outcome is what it "sees," how the model understands the new input, in the context of what it knows.

Another example is the work from the Magenta team at Google, working on building machine learning models that can generate pieces of music by themselves. Such work can revolutionize the way humans use technology in music production.

1.5 Summary

After introducing some of the general theoretical concepts of machine learning, it is time to start diving into some more practical content and talk about how to get started building AI projects as a front-end developer.

CHAPTER 2

TensorFlow.js

TensorFlow.js is an open source JavaScript library for machine learning. It is developed by Google and is a companion library to TensorFlow, in Python.

This tool enables you to build machine learning applications that can run in the browser or in Node.js.

This way, users don't need to install any software or driver. Simply opening a web page allows you to interact with a program.

2.1 Basics of TensorFlow.js

TensorFlow.js is powered by WebGL and provides a high-level layers API for defining models and low-level API (previously deeplearn.js) for linear algebra.

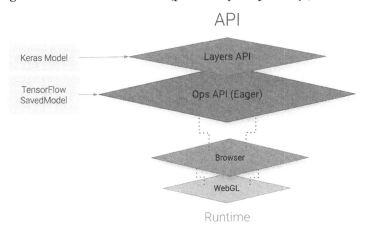

Figure 2-1. *Visual representation of the TensorFlow.js API.*
Source: https://blog.tensorflow.org/2018/03/introducing-tensorflowjs-machine-learning-javascript.html

© Charlie Gerard 2021
C. Gerard, *Practical Machine Learning in JavaScript*,
https://doi.org/10.1007/978-1-4842-6418-8_2

It also supports importing models saved from TensorFlow and Keras.

At the core of TensorFlow is **tensors**. A tensor is a unit of data, a set of values shaped into an array of one or more dimensions. It is similar to multidimensional arrays.

2.1.1 Creating tensors

For example, you imagine the following example 2D array.

Listing 2-1. Example of 2D array

```
const data = [
    [0.456, 0.378, 0.215],
    [0.876, 0.938, 0.276],
    [0.629, 0.287, 0.518]
];
```

The way to transform this into a tensor so it can be used with TensorFlow.js is to wrap it with the built-in method tf.tensor.

Listing 2-2. Creating a tensor out of an array

```
const data = [
    [0.456, 0.378, 0.215],
    [0.876, 0.938, 0.276],
    [0.629, 0.287, 0.518]
];
const dataTensor = tf.tensor(data);
```

Now, the variable dataTensor can be used with other TensorFlow methods to train a model, generate predictions, and so on.

Some extra properties can be accessed in tf.tensor, such as rank, shape, and dtype.

- **rank**: Indicates how many dimensions the tensor contains

- **shape**: Defines the size of each dimension of the data

- **dtype**: Defines the data type of the tensor

Listing 2-3. Logging a tensor's shape, rank, and dtype

```
const tensor = tf.tensor([[1, 2, 3], [4, 5, 6], [7, 8, 9]]);

console.log("shape: ", tensor.shape); // [3,3]
console.log("rank: ", tensor.rank); // 2
console.log("dtype: ", tensor.dtype); // float32
```

In the sample tensor illustrated, the shape returns [3, 3] as we can see 3 arrays containing 3 values.

The rank property prints 2 as we are working with a 2D array. If we had added another dimension to our array, the rank would have been 3.

Finally, the dtype is float32 as this is the default data type.

Tensors can also be created using other data types like bool, int32, complex64, and string dtypes. To do so, we need to pass the shape as second parameter and dtype as a third parameter to tf.tensor.

Listing 2-4. Creating different kinds of tensors

```
const tensor = tf.tensor([[1, 2], [4, 5]], [2,2], "int32");

console.log("shape: ", tensor.shape); // [2,2]
console.log("rank: ", tensor.rank); // 2
console.log("dtype: ", tensor.dtype); // int32
```

In the sample code shown so far, we used `tf.tensor` to create tensors; however, more methods are available to create them with different dimensions.

Depending on the data you are working with, you can use the methods from `tf.tensor1d` to `tf.tensor6d` to create tensors of up to six dimensions.

If the data you are transforming is a multidimensional array of six layers, you can use both `tf.tensor` and `tf.tensor6d`; however, using `tf.tensor6d` makes the code more readable as you can automatically know the amount of dimensions.

Listing 2-5. Creating multidimensional tensors

```
const tensor = tf.tensor6d([
  [
    [
      [
        [[1], [2]],
        [[3], [4]]
      ],
      [
        [[5], [6]],
        [[7], [8]]
      ]
    ]
  ]
]);

// Is the same thing as
```

```
const sameTensor = tf.tensor([
  [
    [
      [
        [[1], [2]],
        [[3], [4]]
      ],
      [
        [[5], [6]],
        [[7], [8]]
      ]
    ]
  ]
]);
```

When creating tensors, you can also pass in a flat array and indicate the shape you would like the tensor to have.

Listing 2-6. Creating tensors from flat arrays

```
const tensor = tf.tensor2d([
  [1, 2, 3],
  [4, 5, 6]
]);

// is the same thing as

const sameTensor = tf.tensor([1, 2, 3, 4, 5, 6], [2, 3]);
```

Once a tensor has been instantiated, it is possible to change its shape using the reshape method.

2.1.2 Accessing data in tensors

Once a tensor is created, you can get its values using `tf.array()` or `tf.data()`.

`tf.array()` returns the multidimensional array of values, and `tf.data()` returns the flattened data.

Listing 2-7. Accessing data in tensors

```
const tensor = tf.tensor2d([[1, 2, 3], [4, 5, 6]]);

const array = tensor.array().then(values => console.log("array: ": values));
// array: [ [1, 2, 3], [4, 5, 6] ]

const data = tensor.data().then(values => console.log("data: ", values));
// data: Float32Array [1, 2, 3, 4, 5, 6];
```

As you can see in the preceding example, these two methods return a promise.

In JavaScript, a promise is a proxy for a value that is not created yet at the time the promise is called. Promises represent operations that have not completed yet, so they are used with asynchronous actions to supply a value at some point in the future when the action has completed.

However, a synchronous version is also provided using `arraySync()` and `dataSync()`.

Listing 2-8. Accessing data in tensors synchronously

```
const tensor = tf.tensor2d([[1, 2, 3], [4, 5, 6]]);

const values = tensor.arraySync();
console.log("values: ": values); // values: [ [1, 2, 3],
[4, 5, 6] ]
```

30

```
const data = tensor.dataSync()
console.log("data: ", values); // data: Float32Array [1, 2, 3,
                                  4, 5, 6];
```

It is not recommended to use them in production applications as they will cause performance issues.

2.1.3 Operations on tensors

In the previous section, we learned that tensors are data structures that allow us to store data in a way TensorFlow.js can work with. We saw how to create them, shape them, and access their values.

Now, let's look into some of the different operations that allow us to manipulate them.

These operations can be organized into categories. Some of them allow you to do arithmetic on a tensor, for example, adding multiple tensors together, other operations focus on doing logical operations such as evaluating if a tensor is greater than another, and others provide a way to do basic maths, like computing the square of all elements in a tensor.

The full list of operations is available at https://js.tensorflow.org/api/latest/#Operations.

Here's an example of how to use these operations.

Listing 2-9. Example of operation on a tensor

```
const tensorA = tf.tensor([1, 2, 3, 4]);
const tensorB = tf.tensor([5, 6, 7, 8]);

const tensor = tf.add(tensorA, tensorB); // [6, 8, 10, 12]

// or

// const tensor = tensorA.add(tensorB);
```

In this example, we're adding two tensors together. If you're looking at the first value of tensorA, which is 1, and the first value of tensorB, which is 5, adding 1 + 5 does result in the number 6, which is the first value of our final tensor.

To be able to use this kind of operations, your tensors have to have the same **shape** but not necessarily the same **rank**.

If you remember from the last few pages, the shape is the amount of values in each dimension of the tensor, when the rank is the amount of dimensions.

Let's illustrate this with another example.

Listing 2-10. Example of operation on a tensor

```
const tensorA = tf.tensor2d([[1, 2, 3, 4]]);
const tensorB = tf.tensor([5, 6, 7, 8]);

const tensor = tf.add(tensorA, tensorB); // [[6, 8, 10, 12],]
```

In this case, tensorA is now a 2D tensor, but tensorB is still one dimensional.

The result of adding the two is now a tensor with the same values as before but with a different number of dimensions.

However, if we try to add multiple tensors with different shapes, it will result in an error.

Listing 2-11. Error generated when using an incorrect shape

```
const tensorA = tf.tensor([1, 2, 3, 4]);
const tensorB = tf.tensor([5, 6, 7]);

const tensor = tf.add(tensorA, tensorB);
// Error: Operands could not be broadcast together with shapes
3 and 4.
```

What this error is telling us is that this operand cannot be used with these two tensors, as one of them has four elements, and the other only three.

Tensors are immutable, so these operations will not mutate the original tensors, but will instead always return a new tf.Tensor.

2.1.4 Memory

Finally, when working with tensors, you need to explicitly clear up memory using dispose() or tf.dispose().

Listing 2-12. Using the dispose method

```
const tensor = tf.tensor([1, 2, 3, 4]);

tensor.dispose();

// or

tf.dispose(tensor);
```

Another way to manage memory is using tf.tidy() when chaining operations.

As tensors are immutable, the result of each operation is a new tensor. To avoid having to call dispose on all the tensors you generate, using tf.tidy() allows you to only keep the last one generated from all your operations and dispose of all the others.

Listing 2-13. Using the tidy method

```
const tensorA = tf.tensor([1, 2, 3, 4]);

const tensor = tf.tidy(() => {
  return tensorA.square().neg();
});

console.log(tensor.dataSync()); // [-1, -4, -9, -16]
```

In this example, the result of square() is going to be disposed, whereas the result of neg() won't as it returns the value of the function.

Now that we have covered what is at the core of TensorFlow.js and how to work with tensors, let's look into the different features offered by the library to get a better idea of what is possible.

2.2 Features

In this subchapter, we are going to explore the three main features currently available in TensorFlow.js. This includes using a pre-trained model; doing transfer learning, which means retraining a model with custom input data; and doing everything in JavaScript, meaning, creating a model, training it, and running predictions, all in the browser.

We will cover these features from the simplest to use to the most complex.

2.2.1 Using a pre-trained model

In the first chapter of this book, we defined the term "model" as a mathematical function that can take new parameters to make predictions based on the data it had been trained with.

If this definition is still a bit confusing to you, hopefully putting it into context while talking about this first feature is going to make it a bit clearer.

In machine learning, to be able to predict an outcome, we need a model. However, it is not necessary to have built the model yourself. It is totally fine to use what is called "pre-trained models."

The term "pre-trained" means that this model has already been trained with a certain type of input data and has been developed for a specific purpose.

For example, you can find some open source pre-trained models focused on object detection and recognition. These models have already been fed with millions of images of objects, have gone through all the training process, and should now have a satisfying level of accuracy when predicting new entities.

Companies or institutions creating these models make them open source so developers can use them in their application and have the opportunity to build machine learning projects much faster.

As you can imagine, the process of gathering data, formatting it, labelling it, experimenting with different algorithms and parameters can take a lot of time, so being able to substitute this work by using a pre-trained model frees up a lot of time to focus on building applications.

Pre-trained models currently available to use with TensorFlow.js include body segmentation, pose estimation, object detection, image classification, speech command recognition, and sentiment analysis.

Using a pre-trained model in your application is relatively easy.

In the following code sample, we're going to use the mobilenet object detection model to predict an entity in a new image.

Listing 2-14. Classifying an image using the mobilenet model

```
const img = document.getElementById("img");

const model = await mobilenet.load();

const predictions = await model.classify(img);

return predictions;
```

In a real application, this code would need to require the TensorFlow.js library and mobilenet pre-trained model beforehand, but more complete code samples will be shown in the next few chapters as we dive into building actual projects.

The preceding sample starts by getting the HTML element that should contain the image we would like to predict. The next step is to load the mobilenet model asynchronously.

Models can be of a rather large size, sometimes a few megabytes, so they need to be loaded using `async/await` to make sure that this operation is fully finished by the time you run the prediction.

Once the model is ready, you can call the `classify()` method on it, in which you pass your HTML element, that will return an array of predictions.

In an example where you would be using an image of a cat, the output of the prediction would look similar to this.

Figure 2-2. *A picture of a cat*

```
▼(3) [{…}, {…}, {…}]  ℹ
  ▶0: {className: "tiger cat", probability: 0.6938019394874573}
  ▶1: {className: "tabby, tabby cat", probability: 0.21018236875534058}
  ▶2: {className: "bow tie, bow-tie, bowtie", probability: 0.01766340807080269}
   length: 3
  ▶__proto__: Array(0)
```

Figure 2-3. *Result of the image classification from the mobilenet model applied to the picture of the cat earlier*

The result of using `classify()` is always an array of three objects containing two keys: *className* and *probability*.

The className is a string containing the label, or class, the model has categorized the new input in, based on the data it has been previously trained with.

The probability is a float value between 0 and 1 that represents the likelihood of the input data belonging to the className, 0 being not likely and 1 being very likely.

They are organized in descending order so the first object in the array is the prediction the most likely to be true.

In the output earlier, the model predicts that the image contains a "tiger cat" with 70% likelihood.

The rest of the predictions have a probability value that drops quite significantly, with 21% chance that it contains a "tabby cat" and about 0.02% probability that it contains a "bow tie."

In general, you would focus on the first value returned in the predictions, as it has the highest probability; however, 70% is actually not that high.

In machine learning, you aim to have the highest probability possible when using predictions. In this case, we only predicted the existence of a cat in an image, but in real applications, you can imagine that a 30% chance of having predicted an incorrect output is not acceptable.

To improve this, in general, we would do what is called "hyperparameter tuning" and retrain the model.

Hyperparameter tuning is the process of tweaking and optimizing the parameters used when generating a model. It could be adding layers in a neural network, changing the batch size, and so on and seeing the effect of these changes on the performance and accuracy of the model.

However, when using a pre-trained model, you would not have the ability to do this, as the only thing you have access to is the output model, not the code written to create it.

This is one of the limits that comes with using pre-trained models.

When using these models, you have no control over how they were created and how to modify them. You usually don't have access to the dataset used in the training process, so you cannot be sure that it will meet the requirements for your application.

Besides, you take the risk of inheriting the company's or institution's biases.

If your application involves implementing facial recognition and you decide to use an open source pre-trained model, you cannot be sure this model was trained on a diverse dataset of people. As a result, you may be unknowingly supporting certain biases by using them.

There had been issues in the past with facial recognition models only performing well on white people, leaving behind a huge group of users with darker skin.

Even though work has been done to fix this, we regularly hear about machine learning models making biased predictions because the data used to train them was not diverse enough.

If you decide to use a pre-trained model in a production application, I believe it's important to do some research beforehand.

2.2.2 Transfer learning

The second feature available in TensorFlow.js is called "transfer learning."

Transfer learning is the ability to reuse a model developed for a task, as the starting point for a model on a second task.

If you imagine an object recognition model that has been pre-trained on a dataset you don't have access to, the function at the core of the model is to recognize entities in images. Using transfer learning, you can leverage this model to create a new one which function will be the same, but trained using your custom input data.

Transfer learning is a way to generate a semicustomized model. You are still not able to modify the model itself, but you can feed it your own data, which can improve the accuracy of the predictions.

If we reuse our example from the previous section where we used a pre-trained model to detect the presence of a cat in a picture, we could see that the prediction came back with the label "tiger cat." This means that the model was trained with images labelled as such, but what if we want to detect something very different, like Golden Wattles (Australian flowers)?

The first step would be to search for the list of classes the model can predict and see if it contains these flowers. If it does, it means the model can be used directly, just like shown in the previous section.

However, if it was not trained with images of Golden Wattles, it will not be able to detect them until we generate a new model using transfer learning.

To do this, a part of the code is similar to the samples shown in the previous section as we still need to start with the pre-trained model, but we introduce some new logic.

We need to start by importing a K-nearest neighbors classifier to our application, alongside TensorFlow.js and the mobilenet pre-trained model.

Listing 2-15. Importing TensorFlow.js, mobilenet, and a KNN classifier

```
<script src="https://cdn.jsdelivr.net/npm/@tensorflow/tfjs/
dist/tf.min.js"></script>

<script src="https://cdn.jsdelivr.net/npm/@tensorflow-models/
mobilenet@1.0.0"></script>

<script src="https://cdn.jsdelivr.net/npm/@tensorflow-models/
knn-classifier"></script>
```

Doing so gives us access to a knnClassifier object.
To instantiate it, we need to call the create method.

Listing 2-16. Instantiating the KNN classifier

```
const classifier = knnClassifier.create();
```

This classifier is going to be used to enable us to make predictions from custom input data, instead of only using the pre-trained model.

The main steps in this process involve doing what is called **inference** on the model, which means applying the mobilenet model to new data, adding these examples to the classifier, and predicting the classes.

Listing 2-17. Adding example data to a KNN classifier

```
const img = await webcam.capture();
const activation = model.infer(img, 'conv_preds');
classifier.addExample(activation, classId);
```

The preceding code sample is incomplete, but we will cover it more in depth in the following chapters, when we focus on implementing transfer learning in an application.

The most important here is to understand that we save an image from the webcam feed in a variable, use it as new data on the model, and add this as an example with a class (label) to the classifier, so the end result is a model that is able to recognize not only the data similar to the one used in the initial training process of the mobilenet model but also our new samples.

Feeding a single new image and example to the classifier is not enough for it to be able to accurately recognize our new input data; therefore, this step has to be repeated multiple times.

Once you think your classifier is ready, you can predict inputs like this.

Listing 2-18. Classifying a new image

```
const img = await webcam.capture();
const activation = model.infer(img, 'conv_preds');
const result = await classifier.predictClass(activation);
```

```
const classes = ["A", "B", "C"];
const prediction = classes[result.label];
```

The first steps are the same, but instead of adding the example to the classifier, we use the `predictClass` method to return a result of what it thinks the new input is.

We will go more in depth about transfer learning in the next chapter.

2.2.3 Creating, training, and predicting

Finally, the third feature allows you to create the model yourself, run the training process, and use it, all in JavaScript.

This feature is more complex than the two previous ones but will be covered more deeply in Chapter 5, when we build an application using a model we will create ourselves.

It is important to know that creating a model yourself requires a trial and error approach.

There is not a single way to solve a problem, and if you decide to go down that path, you will need to experiment a lot with different algorithms, parameters, and so on.

The most common type of model used is a sequential model that you can create with a list of layers.

An example of such model could look like this.

Listing 2-19. Creating a model

```
const model = tf.sequential();

model.add(tf.layers.conv2d({
        inputShape: [28, 28, 1],
        kernelSize: 5,
        filters: 8,
        strides: 1,
```

```
        activation: 'relu',
        kernelInitializer: 'VarianceScaling'
}));

model.add(tf.layers.maxPooling2d({
        poolSize: [2, 2],
        strides: [2, 2]
}));

model.add(tf.layers.conv2d({
        kernelSize: 5,
        filters: 16,
        strides: 1,
        activation: 'relu',
        kernelInitializer: 'VarianceScaling'
}));
```

We start by instantiating it using `tf.sequential` and add multiple different layers to it.

This step is a bit arbitrary in the sense that choosing the type and number of layers, as well as the parameters passed to the layers, is more of an art than a science.

Your model will probably not be perfect the first time you write it and will require multiple changes before you end up with a result that will be the most performant.

One important thing to keep in mind is to provide an `inputShape` parameter in the first layer of your model to indicate the shape of the data the model is going to be trained on. The subsequent layers do not need it.

After creating the model, the next step is to train it with data. This step is done using the `fit` method.

Listing 2-20. Fitting a model with data

```
await model.fit(data, label, options);
```

42

In general, before calling this method, you split your data into batches to train your model little by little. An entire dataset is often too big to be used at once, so dividing it into batches is important.

The options parameter passed into the function is an object containing information about the training process. You can specify the number of **epochs**, which is when the entire dataset is passed through the neural network, and also the batch size, which represents the number of training examples present in a single batch.

As the dataset is split up in batches passed in the `fit` method, we also need to think about the number of **iterations** needed to train the model with the full dataset.

For example, if our dataset contains 1000 examples and our batch size is 100 examples at a time, it will take 10 iterations to complete 1 epoch.

Therefore, we will need to loop and call our `fit` method 10 times, updating the batched data each time.

Once the model is fully trained, it can be used for predictions using the `predict` method.

Listing 2-21. Predicting

```
const prediction = model.predict(data);
```

There is more to cover about this feature, but we will look into it further with our practical example in the next few chapters.

CHAPTER 3

Building an image classifier

In this chapter, we are going to dive deeper into the features of TensorFlow.js by building a couple of web applications that detect objects in images.

There will be more complete code samples with explanations, so you get a better understanding of how to implement machine learning into your projects.

3.1 Using a pre-trained model

The first project we are going to build is a quick game in which you are prompted to find specific objects around you, take a picture of them using your device's camera, and check if the machine learning model recognizes them.

© Charlie Gerard 2021
C. Gerard, *Practical Machine Learning in JavaScript*,
https://doi.org/10.1007/978-1-4842-6418-8_3

The output is going to be as follows:

Figure 3-1. *Snapshot of the image classification project*

At the core of this project is the same object detection model we talked about previously, called **mobilenet**.

This model is pre-trained using the open source ImageNet database made of images organized in 1000 different classes.

What this means is that the model is able to recognize 1000 different objects based on the data it has been trained with.

To start this project, we need to import both TensorFlow.js and the mobilenet model.

There are two ways to do this. Either you can import them using script tags in your HTML file.

Listing 3-1. Importing TensorFlow.js and mobilenet

```
<script src="https://cdn.jsdelivr.net/npm/@tensorflow/tfjs/
dist/tf.min.js"></script>
```

```
<script src="https://cdn.jsdelivr.net/npm/@tensorflow-models/
mobilenet@1.0.0"></script>
```

Or, if you are using a front-end framework, for example, React.js, you can install TensorFlow.js in your dependencies and then import it in a JavaScript file.

In your terminal:

Listing 3-2. Installing the TensorFlow.js and mobilenet modules

```
npm install @tensorflow/tfjs @tensorflow-models/mobilenet
```

```
yarn add @tensorflow/tfjs @tensorflow-models/mobilenet
```

In your JavaScript file:

Listing 3-3. Importing the modules

```
import "@tensorflow/tfjs";
```

```
Import "@tensorflow-models/mobilenet";
```

Importing these two files gives us access to the `tf` and `mobilenet` objects.

The first step we need to take is **load the model** in the app.

Listing 3-4. Loading the model

```
async function app(){
      const model = await model.load();
}
```

```
▼ e {version: "1.00", alpha: "1.00", normalizationOffset: t, model: t} ⓘ
    version: "1.00"
    alpha: "1.00"
  ▼ normalizationOffset: t
      rank: (...)
      isDisposed: (...)
      kept: false
      isDisposedInternal: false
    ▶ shape: []
      dtype: "float32"
      size: 1
    ▶ strides: []
    ▶ dataId: {}
      id: 0
      rankType: "0"
    ▶ __proto__: Object
  ▼ model: t
      modelVersion: (...)
      inputNodes: (...)
      outputNodes: (...)
      inputs: (...)
      outputs: (...)
      weights: (...)
      modelUrl: "https://tfhub.dev/google/imagenet/mobilenet_v1_100_224/classification/1/model.json?tfjs-format=file"
    ▶ loadOptions: {fromTFHub: true}
      version: "undefined.undefined"
    ▶ handler: t {DEFAULT_METHOD: "POST", weightPathPrefix: undefined, onProgress: undefined, path: "https://tfhub.d…
    ▶ artifacts: {modelTopology: {…}, weightSpecs: Array(72), weightData: ArrayBuffer(16908084), userDefinedMetadata…
    ▶ executor: t {graph: {…}, compiledMap: Map(1), _weightMap: {…}, SEPERATOR: ",", _outputs: Array(1), …}
    ▶ __proto__: Object
  ▶ __proto__: Object
```

Figure 3-2. *Console output of a model*

Models being pretty heavy files, they can take a few seconds to load
and therefore should be loaded using `async/await`.

If you are curious to know what this object contains, you can log it and
look at its properties.

Please remember that you do not have to understand every property in
the object to be able to use it.

One of the properties that could be interesting, however, is the *inputs*
property in *model*.

```
▼ model: t
    modelVersion: (...)
  ▶ inputNodes: Array(1)
    outputNodes: (...)
  ▼ inputs: Array(1)
    ▼ 0:
        name: "images"
      ▶ shape: (4) [-1, 224, 224, 3]
        dtype: "float32"
      ▶ __proto__: Object
      length: 1
    ▶ __proto__: Array(0)
```

Figure 3-3. *Console output of a model*

This property shows us the type of input used to train the model. In this case, we can see that images were used, which makes sense considering this is an object detection model. More importantly, we can see the shape of the data used in the training process.

The shape attribute reveals the value [-1, 224, 224, 3], which means that the images fed to the model were RGB images (the value 3 at the end of the array represents the number or channels) of size 224*224 pixels.

This value is particularly interesting for the next part of this chapter, where we will look at doing transfer learning with the mobilenet model.

Feel free to explore the model further.

The next step to build this application is to allow TensorFlow.js to have access to the input from the webcam to be able to run predictions and detect objects.

As our project uses the device's webcam, we have a <video> element in our HTML.

In JavaScript, we need to access this element and use one of TensorFlow's methods to create an object from the data API that can capture images as tensors.

Listing 3-5. Instantiating a webcam object

```
const webcamElement = document.getElementsByTagName("video")[0];

const webcam = await tf.data.webcam(webcamElement);
```

These two lines are still part of the setup process of our application. At the moment, we only loaded the model and created this webcam variable that will transform snapshots from the camera to tensors.

Now, to implement the logic, we need to start by adding a simple button to our HTML. It will be used to trigger the image capture on click.

Listing 3-6. Button to capture an image

```
<button class="capture-image">SNAP</button>
```

In our JavaScript file, we need to access this element, use the onclick event listener, and use TensorFlow.js to capture an image, and classify it.

Listing 3-7. Classifying an image

```
const captureButton = document.getElementsByClassName("capture-
image")[0];
captureButton.onclick = async () => {
    const img = await webcam.capture();
    const predictions = await model.classify(img);
    return predictions;
};
```

To capture an image from the video feed, TensorFlow.js has a capture() built-in method that needs to be called on the object previously created using tf.data.webcam.

It allows to transform a single image directly into a tensor so it can then easily be used with other TensorFlow.js operations.

After capturing an image, we generate predictions by passing it in mobilenet.classify.

This will return an array of predictions.

For example, this picture taken of a plastic bottle will return the following array of predictions.

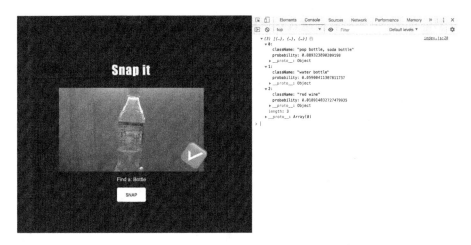

Figure 3-4. *Live object classification*

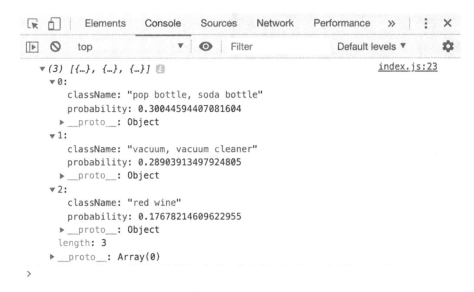

Figure 3-5. *Prediction result printed in the console*

51

As you can see, the first prediction, the one the model is the most confident about, has a label of "pop bottle, soda bottle". It successfully detected the presence of a bottle in the image; however, the probability is really poor, even though it is the correct result.

The fact that the level of confidence in the prediction is only 30% is probably due to the background behind the object. The more complex the background is, the harder it is going to be for the model to be able to find the object in the image and classify it.

This issue is more related to the field of computer vision itself than a framework problem.

As the following image demonstrates, if you try taking the same picture on a clearer background, the quality of the predictions seems to be much better.

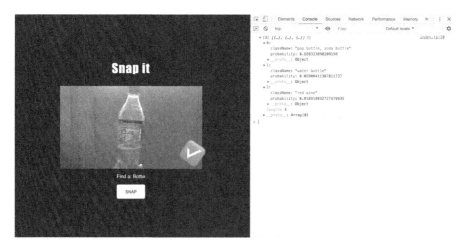

Figure 3-6. *Prediction results on a clearer background*

Not only is the probability much higher, at almost 89%, but the following predictions are also more accurate.

In the first example, the second prediction was "vacuum cleaner", which is far from accurate, but here, it comes back with "water bottle", which is a result much closer to the truth.

This limitation is definitely something you should take into consideration if you are planning on integrating object detection into your application. Thinking about the context in which your project will be used is important to avoid a bad user experience.

Finally, there is one last step in this process. We need to clear up the memory we aren't going to need anymore. Once the image is captured and fed to TensorFlow.js to be classified, we don't need it anymore and therefore should free up the memory it is taking.

To do so, TensorFlow.js provides the `dispose` method that you use like this.

Listing 3-8. Free some memory with the dispose method

```
img.dispose();
```

We've covered the main part of the logic around object detection. However, the first part of the game is to be prompted to find specific objects to take a picture of.

This code is not TensorFlow.js specific and can be a simple UI that asks you to find a new object every time you've successfully found the previous one.

However, if your UI asks you to find a mobile phone, you would need to make sure the model has been trained with pictures of mobile phones so it can detect the correct object.

Luckily, a list of the classes of objects that can be recognized by the mobilenet model is available in the repository at `https://github.com/tensorflow/tfjs-models/blob/master/mobilenet/src/imagenet_classes.ts`.

If you import this list in your application, your code can then loop through this object of 1000 entries and display a random one in the UI to ask the user to find this object around them.

As this code does not involve the use of the TensorFlow.js library, we are not going to cover it in this book.

However, if you'd like to see how all the code samples shown earlier fit together, here is what it should look like.

Listing 3-9. Complete HTML file

```html
<html lang="en">
  <head>
    <meta charset="UTF-8" />
    <meta name="viewport" content="width=device-width, initial-
    scale=1.0"
    />
    <script src="https://cdn.jsdelivr.net/npm/@tensorflow/tfjs/
    dist/tf.min.js"></script>
    <script src="https://cdn.jsdelivr.net/npm/@tensorflow-
    models/mobilenet@1.0.0"></script>
    <title>Snap it</title>
  </head>
  <body>
    <main>
      <section class="content">
        <h1>Snap it</h1>
        <video></video>
        <button>SNAP</button>
      </section>
    </main>
  </body>

  <script src="index.js"></script>
</html>
```

Listing 3-10. Complete JavaScript code

```
async function app() {
  const webcamElement = document.getElementsByTagName("video")[0];
  const model = await mobilenet.load();

  const webcam = await tf.data.webcam(webcamElement);
  const captureButton = document.getElementsByTagName("button")
  [0];

  captureButton.onclick = async () => {
    const img = await webcam.capture();

    const predictions = await model.classify(img);
    img.dispose();
    return predictions;
  };
}
app();
```

In this subchapter, we've used object detection to build a small game, but it can be used for very different applications.

3.2 Transfer learning

Using a pre-trained model is really useful, allowing you to build projects very fast, but you can quickly reach its limits if you find yourself needing something more customized.

In this subchapter, we are going to leverage some parts of the code we wrote in the last few pages, and adapt them to use custom input data.

We're going to collect custom data samples from our webcam to build a model that can recognize our head movements. This can then be used as potential controls for interfaces, so you could imagine using this model to scroll a web page by tilting your head up and down or using the same movements to navigate a map.

This project is going to focus on training the model to recognize new samples and testing its predictions.

The code you'll read in the next few pages will produce an interface with buttons to collect new data and an additional button to run the predictions. The result will be shown on the page for you to verify the accuracy of your model.

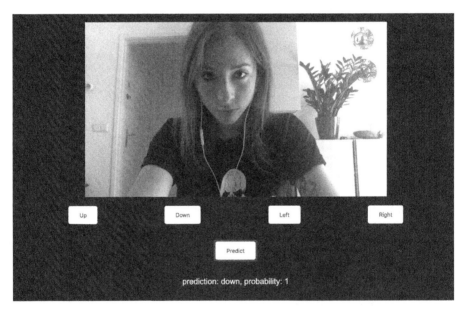

Figure 3-7. *Classifying head movements from webcam input*

Figure 3-8. *Classifying head movements from webcam input*

As you can see in the preceding screenshots, head movements between down and left are predicted accurately.

To get started, we need to import TensorFlow.js, the mobilenet module, and a K-nearest neighbors classifier.

Listing 3-11. Importing TensorFlow.js, mobilenet, and a KNN classifier

```
<script src="https://cdn.jsdelivr.net/npm/@tensorflow/tfjs/
dist/tf.min.js"></script>

<script src="https://cdn.jsdelivr.net/npm/@tensorflow-models/
mobilenet@1.0.0"></script>

<script src="https://cdn.jsdelivr.net/npm/@tensorflow-models/
knn-classifier"></script>
```

As mentioned earlier, we also need to have a video element to show the webcam feed, some buttons, and a paragraph to display the result of our prediction.

Listing 3-12. HTML elements needed for this project

```
<video class="webcam"></video>

<section class="buttons">
     <button>Up</button>
     <button>Down</button>
     <button>Left</button>
     <button>Right</button>
</section>

<section class="buttons">
     <button class="predict">Predict</button>
</section>

<p class="prediction"></p>
```

In a JavaScript file, we need to write the logic that will collect a sample from the webcam when we click the buttons and feed it to the KNN classifier.

Before we dive into the logic, we need to start by instantiating a few variables for the classifier, the model, and the webcam.

Listing 3-13. Instantiating the classifier, loading the model, and preparing the webcam object

```
const classifier = knnClassifier.create();
const net = await mobilenet.load();
const webcam = await tf.data.webcam(webcamElement);
```

On the last line, the webcamElement variable refers to the HTML video element you would get by using standard Document interface methods such as getElementsByClassName.

To implement the logic, we can create a new function we are going to call addExample. This function is going to capture an image from the webcam, transform it into a tensor, retrain the mobilenet model with the image tensor and its label, add that example to the KNN classifier, and dispose of the tensor.

This may sound like a lot but the code needed to do this is actually no more than a few lines.

Listing 3-14. addExample function to retrain the model with custom inputs

```
const addExample = async classId => {
      const img = await webcam.capture();

      const activation = net.infer(img, "conv_preds");

      classifier.addExample(activation, classId);

      img.dispose();
};
```

The second line allows us to capture a single image from the webcam feed and transform it directly into a tensor, so it can be used with other TensorFlow.js methods right away.

The activation variable holds the value of the mobilenet model retrained with the new image tensor from the webcam, using one of its activation functions called "conv_preds".

An activation function is a function that helps a neural network learn complex patterns in data.

The next step is to use the result of retraining the model and add it as an example to our classifier, with a class ID so it can map the new sample to its label.

In machine learning, even though we usually think of labels as strings, for example, in our case "Right", "Left", and so on, during the training process, these labels are actually swapped with their index in an array of labels.

If our classes are `["up", "down", "left", "right"]`, the class ID when we train the model to recognize our head moving down would be 1 as "down" is the second element in our array.

Finally, we dispose of the image tensor once it has been used, to free up some memory.

This `addExample` method needs to be triggered when we click one of our four buttons.

Listing 3-15. Looping through the buttons elements to attach an onclick event listener that will trigger the addExample function

```
for (var i = 0; i < buttons.length; i++) {
    if (buttons[i] !== predictButton) {
      let index = i;
      buttons[i].onclick = () => addExample(index);
    }
}
```

Considering that the `buttons` variable holds the buttons elements present in the DOM, we want to trigger our `addExample` function on all buttons except the one used to run the predictions.

We pass the button index to the function, so when we click the "Up" button, for example, the class ID will be 0.

This way, every time we click one of our four buttons, an example will be added to the classifier, with the corresponding class ID.

Once we have retrained our model a few times, we can click the predict button to run live predictions.

Listing 3-16. Calling the runPredictions function when clicking the predict button

```
predictButton.onclick = () => runPredictions();
```

This `runPredictions` function will repeat similar steps to the ones explained earlier; however, instead of adding the examples to the KNN classifier, it will trigger the `predictClass` method to classify live input from the webcam, based on the training process we just went through.

Listing 3-17. The runPredictions function

```
async function runPredictions() {
    while (true) {
      if (classifier.getNumClasses() > 0) {
        const img = await webcam.capture();
        const activation = net.infer(img, "conv_preds");
        const result = await classifier.predictClass(activation);

        predictionParagraph.innerText = `
          prediction: ${classes[result.label]},
          probability: ${result.confidences[result.label]}`;

        img.dispose();
      }

      await tf.nextFrame();
    }
}
```

In the preceding sample, we wrap the logic inside a `while` loop because we want to continuously predict the input from the webcam; however, you could also replace it with an `onclick` event if you would like to get predictions only after clicking an element.

If the classifier has been trained with new samples, we repeat the two steps of capturing an image from the webcam and using it with the mobilenet model.

Listing 3-18. Steps repeated between training the classifier and running the predictions

```
const img = await webcam.capture();
const activation = net.infer(img, "conv_preds");
```

We then pass this data in the `predictClass` method called on the KNN classifier to predict its label.

The result from calling this method is an object containing a `classIndex`, a `label,` and an object called `confidences`.

```
▼ {classIndex: 3, label: "3", confidences: {…}}
    classIndex: 3
    label: "3"
  ▼ confidences:
      0: 0
      1: 0
      2: 0
      3: 1
    ▶ __proto__: Object
  ▶ __proto__: Object
```

Figure 3-9. *Output of the classification in the console*

In this case, I was tilting my head to the right, so the `classIndex` and `label` come back with a value of 3, as the button to train the model to recognize this gesture was the last of 4.

The `confidences` object shows us the probability of the predicted label. The value of 1 means that the model is very confident that the gesture recognized is the correct one.

The probability value can vary between 0 and 1.

After getting the result from the prediction, we dispose of the image to free up some memory.

Finally, we call `tf.nextFrame()` to wait for `requestAnimationFrame` to complete before running this code again and predicting the class of the next frame.

Here is how the code would work altogether.

Listing 3-19. Complete HTML code

```
<html lang="en">
  <head>
    <meta charset="UTF-8" />
    <meta name="viewport" content="width=device-width, initial-
    scale=1.0"
     />
    <title>Transfer learning</title>
    <script src="https://cdn.jsdelivr.net/npm/@tensorflow/tfjs/
    dist/tf.min.js"></script>
    <script src="https://cdn.jsdelivr.net/npm/@tensorflow-
    models/mobilenet@1.0.0"></script>
    <script src="https://cdn.jsdelivr.net/npm/@tensorflow-
    models/knn-classifier"></script>
  </head>
  <body>
    <main>
      <section class="content">
        <video class="webcam"></video>
        <section class="buttons">
          <button>Up</button>
          <button>Down</button>
          <button>Left</button>
          <button>Right</button>
        </section>
```

```
        <section class="buttons">
          <button class="predict">Predict</button>
        </section>
        <p class="prediction"></p>
      </section>
    </main>

    <script src="index.js"></script>
  </body>
</html>
```

Listing 3-20. Complete JavaScript code

```
const webcamElement = document.getElementsByClassName("webcam")
[0];
const buttons = document.getElementsByTagName("button");
const predictButton = document.getElementsByClassName(
"predict")[0];
const classes = ["up", "down", "left", "right"];
const predictionParagraph = document.getElementsByClassName
("prediction")[0];
async function app() {
  const classifier = knnClassifier.create();
  const net = await mobilenet.load();
  const webcam = await tf.data.webcam(webcamElement);

  const addExample = async classId => {
    const img = await webcam.capture();
    const activation = net.infer(img, "conv_preds");
    classifier.addExample(activation, classId);
    img.dispose();
  };
```

```
  for (var i = 0; i < buttons.length; i++) {
    if (buttons[i] !== predictButton) {
      let index = i;
      buttons[i].onclick = () => addExample(index);
    }
  }

  predictButton.onclick = () => runPredictions();

  async function runPredictions() {
    while (true) {
      if (classifier.getNumClasses() > 0) {
        const img = await webcam.capture();
        const activation = net.infer(img, "conv_preds");
        const result = await classifier.
        predictClass(activation);

        predictionParagraph.innerText = `
            prediction: ${classes[result.label]},
            probability: ${result.confidences[result.label]}`;

        img.dispose();
      }
      await tf.nextFrame();
    }
  }
}
app();
```

Using transfer learning allows us to retrain a model really fast to fit tailored inputs. In only a few lines of code, we are able to create a customized image classification model.

Depending on the new input data you feed it, you might have to add more or less new examples to get an accurate prediction, but it will always be faster than gathering a full new labelled dataset and creating your own machine learning model from scratch.

CHAPTER 4

Text classification and sentiment analysis

In the previous chapter, we focused on using image data to learn more about machine learning and build an image classifier. In this chapter, we are going to talk about using text data, cover a few concepts of natural language processing, and build a few experiments around sentiment analysis.

4.1 What is sentiment analysis?

Sentiment analysis, also sometimes referred to as sentiment classification, opinion mining, or emotion AI, is the process of interpreting and categorizing emotions expressed in a piece of text to determine the overall sentiment of the person writing it – either positive, negative, or neutral.

It uses natural language processing to identify, extract, and study affective states and subjective information.

Natural language processing, or NLP, is a branch of artificial intelligence which objective is to program computers to process, analyze, and make sense of natural language data.

Giving computers the ability to understand the nuances of human language is a complicated task. It is not only about identifying and extracting keywords in a sentence, but about analyzing and interpreting the meaning behind those words, for example, being able to recognize figures of speech, detect irony, and so on.

© Charlie Gerard 2021
C. Gerard, *Practical Machine Learning in JavaScript*,
https://doi.org/10.1007/978-1-4842-6418-8_4

In this chapter, we will mainly focus on classifying pieces of text data into three categories: positive, negative, and neutral, as well as looking into toxicity detection.

Before diving into how to implement sentiment analysis in JavaScript with TensorFlow.js, let's try to understand more about the mechanics of this technique.

4.2 How does natural language processing work?

The way we express ourselves carries a lot of contextual information. From our selection of words to our tone, the extent of our vocabulary, and the way we construct our sentences, human language is extremely complex but also rich enough to reveal a lot about us.

To allow computers to develop an understanding of language and its intricacies, natural language processing uses a few different techniques and algorithms. Let's start by defining some concepts.

4.2.1 Common concepts – Basics of NLP

Before diving into how to implement some natural language processing in JavaScript, let's cover some basic concepts.

Bag-of-words

Bag-of-words is a model you will probably come across if you decide to do some extra research on NLP as it is quite commonly used.

It is a simplifying representation used to count the occurrence of all words in a piece of text, disregarding grammar.

This approach seems a bit simplistic as it does not take into consideration any semantic meaning and context, but it intends to add some weight to different terms in a text, based on how often they are used. This information is then used as features for training a classifier.

This process is also sometimes referred to as **vectorization**, as it aims to turn pieces of text into fixed-length vectors.

Concepts without examples can be difficult to understand, so let's use the following four sentences to see how the Bag-of-words model would apply.

Let's imagine we want to be able to detect if a piece of text is spam or not, and we have

- Win millions of dollars

- Win a Tesla

- Request for help

- Help millions of developers

The first step is to determine what is called our **vocabulary** or **corpus**, meaning the set of all words we're going to work with, which in our case is

- Win

- Millions

- Of

- Dollars

- A

- Tesla

- Request

- For

- Help

- Developers

Once we have our full vocabulary, we can start counting occurrences of each word.

Table 4-1. *Table representing the occurrences of each word in the preceding list*

Document	Win	Millions	Of	Dollars	A	Tesla	Request	For	Help	Developers
Win millions of dollars	1	1	1	1	0	0	0	0	0	0
Win a Tesla	1	0	0	0	1	0	0	0	0	0
Request for help	0	0	0	0	0	0	1	1	1	0
Help millions of developers	0	1	1	0	0	0	0	0	1	1

Using this representation of the data, we're able to create the following vectors:

- **Win millions of dollars**: [1, 1, 1, 1, 0, 0, 0, 0, 0, 0]
- **Win a Tesla**: [1, 0, 0, 0, 1, 0, 0, 0, 0, 0]
- **Request for help**: [0, 0, 0, 0, 0, 0, 1, 1, 1, 0]
- **Help millions of developers**: [0, 1, 1, 0, 0, 0, 0, 0, 1, 1]

These vectors can then be used as features to train an algorithm.

The two first sentences ("Win millions of dollars" and "Win a Tesla") could be labelled as "spam" and the two last ("Request for help" and "Help millions of developers") as "non-spam".

As a result, the dataset to be used to train an algorithm could look something like the following.

Table 4-2. *Table representing the occurrences of each word in a spammy phrase vs. a non-spammy phrase*

Label	Win	Millions	Of	Dollars	A	Tesla	Request	For	Help	Developers
Spam	1	1	1	1	0	0	0	0	0	0
Spam	1	0	0	0	1	0	0	0	0	0
Non-spam	0	0	0	0	0	0	1	1	1	0
Non-spam	0	1	1	0	0	0	0	0	1	1

Considering that similar kinds of words are used in similar documents, the bag-of-words approach can help us determine the likelihood of a sentence being spam or not, based on our previous example dataset.

If the word "win" is often contained in a text labelled as spam, the probability of a new sentence such as "Win the trip of your dreams" being spam is higher than the probability of another sentence like "Feedback on performance".

It is important to notice that the order of the words in the text does not matter; only the amount of times these words are used.

In real applications, the dataset should be much larger, containing a more diverse corpus, to increase the accuracy of the predictions.

Tokenization

In natural language processing, two common types of tokenization include sentence tokenization and word tokenization.

Sentence tokenization, also called sentence segmentation, is the process of dividing a string into its component sentences. One way to do this is to split sentences whenever we see a full stop (.).

For example, a paragraph such as

"*13th* is a 2016 American documentary film by director Ava DuVernay. The film explores the "intersection of race, justice, and mass incarceration in the United States;" it is titled after the Thirteenth Amendment to the United States Constitution, adopted in 1865, which abolished slavery throughout the United States and ended involuntary servitude except as a punishment for conviction of a crime."

would be split into the following two sentences:

1. "13th is a 2016 American documentary film by director Ava DuVernay"

2. "The film explores the "intersection of race, justice, and mass incarceration in the United States;" it is titled after the Thirteenth Amendment to the United States Constitution, adopted in 1865, which abolished slavery throughout the United States and ended involuntary servitude except as a punishment for conviction of a crime."

Word tokenization, also called word segmentation, is the process of dividing a string into its component words. This can be used by splitting a sentence using a space character as the divider.

For example, our first sentence earlier, "13th is a 2016 American documentary film by director Ava DuVernay", would result in the following output.

Listing 4-1. Example array representing the output of word tokenization on the sentence "13th is a 2016 American documentary film by director Ava DuVernay"

```
["13th", "is", "a", "2016", "American", "documentary", "film",
"by", "director", "Ava", "DuVernay"]
```

Text lemmatization and stemming

Text lemmatization and stemming are techniques to reduce inflectional forms of a word to a common base form.

As related words can have similar meanings, these tools help reduce them to a single one.

For example:

- "Eat", "Eats", "Eating" becomes "Eat".

- "Computer", "Computers", "Computer's" becomes "Computer".

The result of this mapping would look something like this:

"They are all **eating** in front of their **computers**" => "They are all **eat** in front of their **computer**".

This kind of technique is helpful for use cases where we would want to find results for more than an exact input, for example, with search engines.

When we execute a search, we generally are interested in getting relevant results, not only for the exact search terms that we used but also for other possible forms of these words.

For example, if I run a search using the words "Hike Europe", I'm also interested in results that will have the word "hikes" and "hiking" or "hikers", and so on.

Stop words

Stop words are words that can add a lot of noise and are considered irrelevant in a text. They are filtered out before or after processing a text.

Examples of stop words include "and", "the", and "a", but there is no definitive list as it will vary based on language and application.

After filtering out a text for stop words, a sentence like "They are meeting at the station tomorrow at 10am" would end up being ["They", "are", "meeting", "station", "tomorrow", "10am"].

As we can see, the sentence did not lose any meaning after removing the stop words.

As machine learning operations can be time-consuming, removing words that do not change the semantic meaning of a text can improve performance without impacting negatively the accuracy of the predictions.

4.3 Implementing sentiment analysis in TensorFlow.js

Now that we have covered some of the basics of natural language processing, let's work on a couple of applications implementing sentiment analysis in JavaScript using TensorFlow.js.

4.3.1 Positive, negative, and neutral

As a first project, let's build an application that can predict the overall sentiment of a piece of text and classify it between three categories: positive, negative, and neutral.

Importing the model

The first thing you need to do, similar to the other projects in the previous chapter, is importing the TensorFlow.js library, either as a script tag or npm package.

Listing 4-2. Importing TensorFlow.js as a script tag in an HTML file

```
<script src='https://cdn.jsdelivr.net/npm/@tensorflow/tfjs'>
</script>
```

Or

Listing 4-3. Importing TensorFlow.js as a package in a JavaScript file

```
const tf = require('@tensorflow/tfjs');
```

Loading the model

Then, we need to load the pre-trained model and its metadata. For this, we can create two different functions.

Listing 4-4. Function named loadModel to load the machine learning model

```
const loadModel = async () => {
  const url = `https://storage.googleapis.com/tfjs-models/tfjs/
  sentiment_cnn_v1/model.json`;
  const model = await tf.loadLayersModel(url);
  return model;
};
```

Listing 4-5. Function named loadMetadata to load the machine learning metadata

```
const loadMetadata = async () => {
  const url = 'https://storage.googleapis.com/tfjs-models/tfjs/
  sentiment_cnn_v1/metadata.json';
  const metadata = await fetch(url);
  return metadata.json();
};
```

Predictions

Now that we have the main tools we need to run the prediction, we also need to write some helper functions that will turn our input text into vectors, like we talked about in the previous section of this chapter.

Input text cannot be fed to an algorithm as a string, as machine learning models primarily work with numbers, so let's look into how to execute vectorization in JavaScript.

To turn a string into a fixed-length vector, we need to start by breaking it down into an array which elements will be all the substrings.

Listing 4-6. Code sample to vectorize a string in JavaScript

```
const text = 'Hello world';
const trimmed = text
  .trim()
  .toLowerCase()
  .replace(/(\.|\,|\!|\?)/g, "")
  .split(" ");
```

This piece of code will turn a string like "I learned a lot from this talk" into ["i", "learned", "a", "lot", "from", "this", "talk"].

We start by calling the trim() function to remove potential whitespace at the beginning and end of the string. We then make everything lowercase, remove all punctuation, and split it into an array of substrings using the space character as separator.

Once this is done, we need to turn this array into an array of numbers using the metadata we loaded just previously.

This metadata is a JSON file with the sample data used to train the model we are loading into our application. It contains about 20,000 words.

The goal of this step is to map each word in our string to an index from the file, with the following code.

Listing 4-7. Code sample to map words to their index in the metadata file

```
const loadMetadata = async () => {
  const metadata = await fetch(
    "https://storage.googleapis.com/tfjs-models/tfjs/sentiment_
    cnn_v1/metadata.json"
  );
```

```
  return metadata.json();
};
const sequence = trimmed.map(async(word) => {
  const metadata = await loadMetadata();
  const wordIndex = metadata.word_index[word];
  if (typeof wordIndex === "undefined") {
    return 2; //oov index
  }
  return wordIndex + metadata.index_from;
});
```

What this code sample does is loop through the array of substrings we created previously and see if each element exists in the metadata. If it does, it sets the variable wordIndex to the index found in the metadata; otherwise, if the word from our input text was not found in the data used to train the model, it sets the value of wordIndex to 2.

This number 2 is going to be our index for **out-of-vocabulary** (OOV) words.

After this step, this sequence variable will look something like the following sample.

Listing 4-8. Sample output produced by the code earlier

```
[13, 12037, 6, 176, 39, 14, 740]
```

These numbers are the indices of each word in our metadata file. As we can see, the number 2 is not present, which means that each word in the sentence "I learned a lot from this talk" was present in the dataset used to train the model.

Before we can use this to run predictions and get the overall sentiment, we need to do one last step of transforming the data.

As explained previously, when training a machine learning model, you need to make sure that the data used has the same shape.

For example, if you were working with images, you could not use images of different sizes (280x280 pixels, then 1200x800 pixels, etc.) in your dataset.

The same principle applies to text data. Our example text "I learned a lot from this talk" has a length of 7; however, our model has been trained with vectors which length were 100.

This value can be found in the metadata.json file as the value of the property max_len.

What this means is that the longest piece of string in the dataset used to train the model contained 100 words.

As we need to work with fixed-length vectors, we need to transform our vector of length 7 to a vector of length 100.

To do this, we need to write a function that will prepend a certain amount of 0s until the length of the vector equals 100.

After the code sample in Listing 4-7, you can write the following function.

Listing 4-9. Function to transform the data and create fixed-length vectors

```
const padSequences = (sequences, metadata) => {
  return sequences.map((seq) => {
    if (seq.length > metadata.max_len) {
      seq.splice(0, seq.length - metadata.max_len);
    }
    if (seq.length < metadata.max_len) {
      const pad = [];
      for (let i = 0; i < metadata.max_len - seq.length; ++i) {
        pad.push(0);
      }
```

```
    seq = pad.concat(seq);
    }
    return seq;
  });
};
```

```
padSequences([sequence], metadata);
```

This function should be used for text data that is less than 100 words long, but what about strings which length exceeds 100?

The process for this case is kind of the opposite, we loop through the array of indices, and when we reach the maximum length, we slice the array and get rid of the rest.

After this process, the array we're going to use to with our machine learning model should look something like the following.

Listing 4-10. Output array after prepending 0s to create a fixed-length vector

```
[0, 0, 0, 0, 0, 0, 0, 0, 0, 0, 0, 0, 0, 0, 0, 0, 0, 0, 0, 0,
0, 0, 0, 0, 0, 0, 0, 0, 0, 0, 0, 0, 0, 0, 0, 0, 0, 0, 0, 0,
0, 0, 0, 0, 0, 0, 0, 0, 0, 0, 0, 0, 0, 0, 0, 0, 0, 0, 0, 0,
0, 0, 0, 0, 0, 0, 0, 0, 0, 0, 0, 0, 0, 0, 0, 0, 0, 0, 0, 0,
0, 0, 0, 0, 0, 0, 0, 0, 0, 13, 12037, 6, 176, 39, 14, 740]
```

As we can see, we still have our seven indices representing our sentence "I learned a lot from this talk, but prepended with the correct amount of 0s to make this vector have a length of 100.

Now that we've transformed our data into the right vector, we can turn it into a tensor, using the `tensor2d` method and use that to predict the sentiment of our input text.

Listing 4-11. Code sample to transform the vector into a tensor and generate predictions

```
const input = tf.tensor2d(paddedSequence, [1, metadata.max_len]);

const prediction = model.predict(input);
const score = prediction.dataSync()[0];
prediction.dispose();
return score;
```

This score will be a float number between 0 and 1. The closest the score is to 0, the more negative it is predicted to be, and the closest to 1, the more positive.

The score for our input text "I learned a lot from this talk" is 0.9912545084953308, which means that the sentiment predicted for it is "positive".

A sentence like "This is really bad" produces a score of 0.007734981831163168, which is "negative".

Complete example

If we want to put this code altogether in an application that would gather input text from users, this is what it could look like.

If we assume we have a simple input field with a button in an HTML file, like so.

Listing 4-12. HTML tags to get text input from users and a button

```
<label for="text">Text</label>
<input type="text" name="text" />
<button>Predict</button>
```

The JavaScript code to run sentiment analysis on the text written by the user would be as follows.

Listing 4-13. JavaScript code to process user input and run predictions

```javascript
const loadMetadata = async () => {
  const metadata = await fetch(
    "https://storage.googleapis.com/tfjs-models/tfjs/sentiment_
    cnn_v1/metadata.json"
  );
  return metadata.json();
};

const loadModel = async () => {
  const url = `https://storage.googleapis.com/tfjs-models/tfjs/
  sentiment_cnn_v1/model.json`;
  const model = await tf.loadLayersModel(url);
  return model;
};

const padSequences = (sequences, metadata) => {
  return sequences.map((seq) => {
    if (seq.length > metadata.max_len) {
      seq.splice(0, seq.length - metadata.max_len);
    }
    if (seq.length < metadata.max_len) {
      const pad = [];
      for (let i = 0; i < metadata.max_len - seq.length; ++i) {
        pad.push(0);
      }
      seq = pad.concat(seq);
    }
    return seq;
  });
};
```

```javascript
const predict = (text, model, metadata) => {
  const trimmed = text
    .trim()
    .toLowerCase()
    .replace(/(\.|\,|\!|\?)/g, "")
    .split(" ");

  const sequence = trimmed.map((word) => {
    const wordIndex = metadata.word_index[word];
    if (typeof wordIndex === "undefined") {
      return 2; //oov_index
    }
    return wordIndex + metadata.index_from;
  });
  const paddedSequence = padSequences([sequence], metadata);
  const input = tf.tensor2d(paddedSequence, [1, metadata.max_
  len]);

  const predictOut = model.predict(input);
  const score = predictOut.dataSync()[0];
  predictOut.dispose();
  return score;
};

const getSentiment = (score) => {
  if (score > 0.66) {
    return `Score of ${score} is Positive`;
  } else if (score > 0.4) {
    return `Score of ${score} is Neutral`;
  } else {
    return `Score of ${score} is Negative`;
  }
};
```

```
const run = async (text) => {
  const model = await loadModel();
  const metadata = await loadMetadata();
  let sum = 0;
  text.forEach(function (prediction) {
    perc = predict(prediction, model, metadata);
    sum += parseFloat(perc, 10);
  });
  console.log(getSentiment(sum / text.length));
};

window.onload = () => {
  const inputText = document.getElementsByTagName("input")[0];
  const button = document.getElementsByTagName("button")[0];
  button.onclick = () => {
    run([inputText.value]);
  };
};
```

In this code sample, I am using the user's input as a single string that will be transformed and used for sentiment analysis. However, if you wanted to split a paragraph into different sentences and run sentiment analysis on each sentence separately, you would need to start by creating a function that breaks the paragraph into an array of sentences.

If you decide to implement this and try sentiment analysis on various pieces of text, you might realize that the accuracy of the prediction is not always the best.

For example, a sentence, like "I really hate this", has a score of 0.9253836274147034, meaning its sentiment is predicted to be "positive", which seems incorrect.

This is mainly due to the fact that the data used to train the model is a set of 25,000 movie reviews from IMDB, an online database of information related to films, TV shows, and so on.

Even though, to humans, a sentence like "I really hate this" seems pretty clearly negative, the machine learning model only looks at the occurrence of every word in the sentence, compared to what it has learned from the training data.

If the words "i", "really", and "this" were found in more sentences and these were labelled as "positive", it overweighs the fact that the word "hate" looks to us as a negative sentiment. This word was probably used in less sentences in the dataset.

All this is to remind you to never rely entirely on predictions generated by a machine learning model. Even though algorithms are much better than humans at processing large amounts of data and extracting patterns from it, predictions should be used as a way to augment the way we make decisions, not replace it completely.

If you wanted to improve these predictions, you could look for other open source datasets or pre-trained models used for sentiment analysis.

4.3.2 Toxicity Classifier

Now that we looked into implementing a sentiment analysis classifier, let's use something a little different that will produce more specified predictions.

In this subchapter, we're going to use TensorFlow's Toxicity Classifier to label pieces of text based on their type of toxicity.

The different labels are

- Insult

- Identity attack

- Obscene

- Severe toxicity

- Sexual explicit

- Threat

- Toxicity

Importing the model

To get started using this model, we need to import the TensorFlow.js library and the pre-trained model for toxicity recognition.

Listing 4-14. Import TensorFlow.js and the Toxicity Classifier in your HTML file using script tags

```
<script src='https://cdn.jsdelivr.net/npm/@tensorflow/tfjs'></
script>
<script src='https://cdn.jsdelivr.net/npm/@tensorflow-models/
toxicity'></script>
```

Or

Listing 4-15. Install and import TensorFlow.js and the Toxicity Classifier in your JavaScript file

```
// In your terminal
npm install @tensorflow/tfjs @tensorflow-models/toxicity

// In your JavaScript file
const toxicity = require('@tensorflow-models/toxicity');
```

Predictions

After importing the tools we need, the code to run the prediction on a piece of text is actually pretty small!

We need to load the model and call the `classify()` function with the sentences we want to run the predictions on as argument, like the following.

Listing 4-16. Loading the model and classifying new sentences

```
toxicity.load().then((model) => {
  const sentences = ['this is really the most useless talk I
  have ever watched.'];

  model.classify(sentences).then((predictions) => {
    return predictions;
  });
});
```

For a sentence like the one shown in the preceding code sample, the predictions return as the following array.

```
▼ (7) [{…}, {…}, {…}, {…}, {…}, {…}, {…}] ⃞
  ▶ 0: {label: "identity_attack", results: Array(1)}
  ▶ 1: {label: "insult", results: Array(1)}
  ▶ 2: {label: "obscene", results: Array(1)}
  ▶ 3: {label: "severe_toxicity", results: Array(1)}
  ▶ 4: {label: "sexual_explicit", results: Array(1)}
  ▶ 5: {label: "threat", results: Array(1)}
  ▶ 6: {label: "toxicity", results: Array(1)}
    length: 7
```

Figure 4-1. *Array of predictions returned by the preceding code sample*

At first, you could think that it means the sentence "this is really the most useless talk I have ever watched" has been predicted to belong to the "identity_attack" label; however, that's not it.

The way the predictions come back with this particular model is as an array of objects that contain data for each label, ordered by alphabetical order.

It can be a bit confusing, as other models used with TensorFlow.js usually produce predictions ordered by score.

To get a better understanding, let's get a deeper look into the predictions array that we logged earlier.

```
▼ (7) [{…}, {…}, {…}, {…}, {…}, {…}, {…}] ▣
  ▼ 0:
      label: "identity_attack"
    ▼ results: Array(1)
      ▼ 0:
          match: false
        ▶ probabilities: Float32Array(2) [0.9993070363998413, 0.0006929246592335403]
        ▶ __proto__: Object
          length: 1
        ▶ __proto__: Array(0)
    ▶ __proto__: Object
  ▼ 1:
      label: "insult"
    ▼ results: Array(1)
      ▼ 0:
          match: true
        ▶ probabilities: Float32Array(2) [0.2846406102180481, 0.7153594493865967]
        ▶ __proto__: Object
          length: 1
        ▶ __proto__: Array(0)
    ▶ __proto__: Object
  ▼ 2:
      label: "obscene"
    ▼ results: Array(1)
      ▼ 0:
          match: false
        ▶ probabilities: Float32Array(2) [0.999549925327301, 0.0004499987990129739]
        ▶ __proto__: Object
          length: 1
        ▶ __proto__: Array(0)
    ▶ __proto__: Object
  ▼ 3:
      label: "severe_toxicity"
    ▼ results: Array(1)
      ▼ 0:
          match: false
        ▶ probabilities: Float32Array(2) [0.9999998807907104, 1.3987082070343604e-7]
        ▶ __proto__: Object
          length: 1
        ▶ __proto__: Array(0)
    ▶ __proto__: Object
```

Figure 4-2. *Detailed view of the array of predictions returned by the preceding code sample*

This screenshot represents the four first entries in the predictions array. As we can see, they are ordered alphabetically by label.

To understand which label is the correct one for the input text, we need to look at the "probabilities" array and the "match" value.

The probabilities array contains two values, the first representing the probability of the label being falsy, meaning the input text not being classified with that label, and the second value representing the probability of the label being truthy, meaning the input text is classified as being this type of toxic content.

The "match" value is a more straightforward representation. If its value is "true", it means the text corresponds to that label; if "false", it doesn't.

Sometimes, the value of "match" is set to "null". This happens when neither of the predictions exceeds the threshold provided.

By default, this threshold is not required and has a value of 0.85. However, it can be set to another value and passed to the model as an argument, like so.

Listing 4-17. Passing a threshold as argument to the model

```
const threshold = 0.7;

toxicity.load(threshold).then((model) => {
  const sentences = [
    "This is really the most useless talk I have ever watched.",
  ];

  model.classify(sentences).then((predictions) => {
    return predictions;
  });
});
```

This threshold is used to determine the value of the "match" property.

If the first value in the "probabilities" array exceeds the threshold, "match" is set to "false"; if instead the second value exceeds the threshold, "match" is set to true. And, as explained before, if none of the probabilities values exceed the threshold, "match" is set to "null".

Labels can also be passed as another argument to the model if you only care about certain ones and not all 7.

For example, if we wanted to detect only text that would be classified with the label "identity_attack", we would be passing this label as well.

Listing 4-18. Passing a label as argument to the model

```
const threshold = 0.7;

// Labels have to be passed as an array, even if you only pass
a single one.
toxicity.load(threshold, ["identity_attack"]).then((model) => {
  const sentences = [
    "This is really the most useless talk I have ever watched.",
  ];

  model.classify(sentences).then((predictions) => {
    return predictions;
  });
});
```

Providing the labels you are only interested in will return filtered predictions.

```
▼ [{…}] 🔢
  ▼ 0:
      label: "identity_attack"
    ▼ results: Array(1)
      ▼ 0:
          match: false
        ▶ probabilities: Float32Array(2) [0.9993070363998413, 0.0006929246592335403]
        ▶ __proto__: Object
          length: 1
      ▶ __proto__: Array(0)
    ▶ __proto__: Object
      length: 1
  ▶ __proto__: Array(0)
```

Figure 4-3. *Predictions array returned after passing a specific label*

Similarly to the sentiment classifier built in the previous section of this chapter, the accuracy of the predictions depends a lot on the data used to train the model.

TensorFlow.js's toxicity model was trained on a dataset of about 2 million user-generated online news comments published from 2015 to 2017.

An interesting aspect of this is that datasets are often originally labelled by humans, meaning people have to go through all the entries and label each of them with a corresponding label based on a set of labels provided.

In the case of the data used for the toxicity model, it means that people had to go through 2 million pieces of text, and label each of them with the label they thought would be the closest to the type of toxicity the comment belonged to, based on the labels "identity_attack", "insult", "obscene", "severe_toxicity", "sexual_explicit", "threat", and "toxicity".

One potential issue with this is that different people have different opinions about what they might classify as an "insult" or not, or what they would label as "toxicity" instead of "severe_toxicity", which adds a certain level of bias into the data that is going to be used to train the model.

So, not only the accuracy of the prediction depends on the quality of the data gathered (the online comments), it also depends on how they were labelled.

If you are in a position where you can inspect the data that was used to train a model you are using in your application, I would really recommend to do it.

Now that we went through a couple of examples of what can be done with sentiment analysis with TensorFlow.js, let's look into some potential applications.

4.4 Applications

A lot of the content we produce and share is text content. From news articles and blog posts to comments, chatbots interactions, social media updates, and so on, this vast amount of text data could offer some really interesting new opportunities, if used with machine learning.

4.4.1 Cognitive assistants and computer therapy

Either it be in the form of chatbots or voice assistants like Siri, certain conversational agents could benefit from integrating sentiment analysis.

In the past few years, some companies have tried to develop systems to provide psychological help and coaching in the form of chatbots.

These companies focus on offering tailored advice and support in the aim of allowing people to do some kind of DIY cognitive behavioral therapy (CBT).

CBT uses structured exercises to encourage a person to question and change their habits of thought. This step-by-step format seems well suited for chatbots.

Companies, like Orexo, Woebot, Pear, and Wysa, personalize their services to each person based on their answers to questions.

Orexo focuses on helping users change their drinking habits by asking a set of questions about current behavioral patterns and tailoring a program based on the answers provided.

Woebot, a chatbot built on Stanford research, aims at making mental healthcare accessible to everyone, by providing personalized expert-crafted tools to learn about yourself and improve your mood whenever you need it.

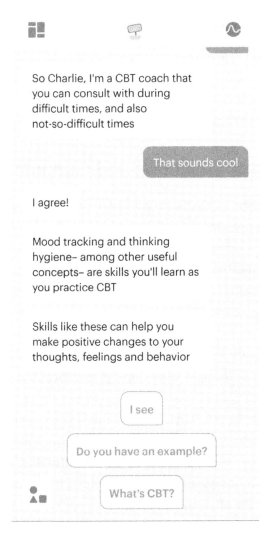

Figure 4-4. *Screenshot of the application Woebot*

Pear Therapeutics is a company at the intersection of biology and software that aims at creating the next generation of therapeutics. It has released two digital services called reSET and reSET-0 that intend to provide support and CBT to people with substance abuse disorders.

Wysa, an AI-based "emotionally intelligent" chatbot, provides self-care exercises organized in packs to help deal with issues such as managing your mood, overcoming loneliness, improving sleep, and so on. Unlike other applications, it also gives you the opportunity to pay for a real session with a professional therapist within the app.

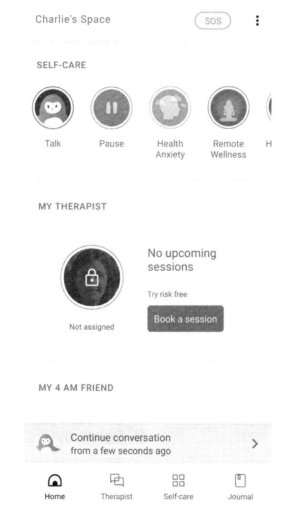

Figure 4-5. *Screenshot of the home screen of the application Wysa*

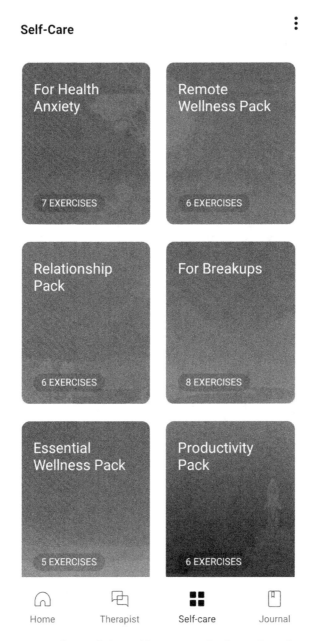

Figure 4-6. *Screenshot of the self-care packs found in the application Wysa*

Some of these applications even got approved by the FDA, the Food and Drug Administration in the United States.

Another one of them is a game called EndeavorRx by Akili Interactive, which trials showed it can help children with ADHD (attention deficit hyperactivity disorder) improve their level of attention. This game was built based on research to deliver sensory and motor stimuli to selectively target and activate specific cognitive neural systems in the brain.

Even though these applications do not replace face-to-face interactions with a therapist, one of their benefits is their constant availability. Getting a daily consultation with a real doctor would be very costly and time-consuming; however, a digital one on your phone can make it easier to keep track of your progress and provide help in urgent moments.

Besides, there are probably not enough clinicians available to help the amount of people in need. For example, the chatbot Woebot exchanges about 4.7 million messages with people per week; there just wouldn't be enough practitioners to handle that.

Even though there is potential in these self-help digital services, it is very important to remember that the technology is not perfect.

As machine learning algorithms get better at analyzing and understanding all information contained in the way we communicate, there can only be improvements in the future, but for now, a lot of these applications have limited abilities and should be used with that in mind.

If this is a space you are interested in, I would highly recommend to try a few of these applications to get a better sense of the features and interactions currently available.

4.4.2 Social media monitoring

Another interesting opportunity is in improving users' interactions on social media by providing some kind of monitoring tool.

If you are regularly using any social media platform like Facebook or Twitter, you are probably familiar with the toxicity of some of the content users decide to share, either in the form of status updates or comments on your posts.

This type of toxic interactions can have a negative psychological impact on people, which could be avoided using sentiment analysis.

At the moment, if anyone is interacting in a toxic way with you on a platform, you do not really have the option to avoid it. You might decide to ignore it, but only after you've seen the content at least once, which often already impacts you negatively.

However, if every piece of content shared was first run by a machine learning model to detect the level of toxicity, social media platforms could provide warnings about the content the user is about to see, and let them decide if they want to view it or not.

The same way content described as "adult content" is often hidden behind some kind of warning, platforms could empower users to make their own decisions.

More recently, Twitter has released warnings on tweets considered to be potentially spreading incorrect information about the disease COVID-19.

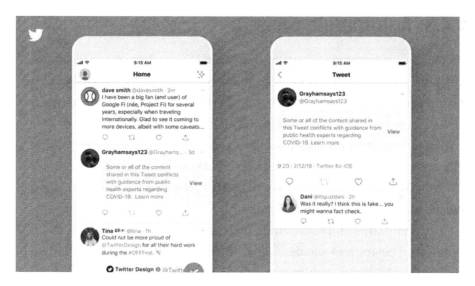

Figure 4-7. *Examples of warnings displayed on tweets that were potentially spreading wrong information. Source:* `www.vox.com/ recode/2020/5/11/21254889/twitter-coronavirus-covid- misinformation-warnings-labels`

Users could still click "View" if they wanted to read the content, but were warned that it was potentially harmful, as it was going against guidance from public health experts.

Additionally, this technique could also be used to attempt to prevent the sharing of toxic content by providing a warning to the person about to post.

When using social media platforms, you could imagine an icon next to the usual "Add emojis" or "Add pictures" icon that would get into an active state if the tweet a user is about to send, or post they are about to share, was classified as being toxic. This would not stop anyone from sharing but would provide people with an opportunity to take a step back and think twice about the impact of their words on other people.

Both of these opportunities do not completely resolve the issue of toxic content on the Internet but use machine learning and sentiment analysis as a help to make the Web a safer place.

4.4.3 Automation tools

There are some situations in our professional lives where some tasks are still done manually that could be automated using sentiment analysis, to free up some time to focus on more interesting challenges. An example of this is around product feedback from customers.

If you work for a product company, you might be familiar with asking your customers for feedback on the product you are building.

This feedback is often stored as a spreadsheet of data, stored in Google Sheets, databases, or other platform.

The company's employees then usually go through all this data to understand customers' needs, complaints, and so on. These tasks can take a lot of time; however, sentiment analysis could be used to apply a first filter to the data and group them by feedback that seems positive, negative, and neutral.

People should still read the data manually to get a better understanding of customers' thoughts, but it could give an idea of the overall sentiment around the product.

Another type of survey where this approach could be useful is in internal company surveys.

When the leadership of a company wants to know how employees are feeling about their work, the culture, or their overall experience, a survey is shared to collect feedback.

Some surveys are rather simple with mainly check boxes where people answer questions or statements by selecting "Strongly agree", "Agree", "Disagree", or "Strongly disagree"; however, some other surveys give employees an opportunity to express themselves further, in their own words.

The latter would be a good use case for sentiment analysis. After collecting feedback from everyone, all the data could be fed to a sentiment analysis model to determine the overall feeling of employees toward the company.

Similarly to the previous example of product surveys, the feedback should still be read and analyzed manually, but getting a first insight over the data may influence the first decisions. If the prediction comes back as overly negative, it is probably important to act on the feedback as soon as possible to avoid getting to the point where employees decide to leave the company.

Finally, another scenario where sentiment analysis could be used for automation is in helping a support team triage tickets based on the toxicity of customer's complaints. This approach could also be used by developer experience teams that usually have to keep track of what is said about a company on social media.

Using a Toxicity Classifier or sentiment analysis classifier to run an initial check on the data can help prioritize which customers' feedback should be dealt with, with more urgency.

All in all, using sentiment analysis as an automation tool does not replace entirely the work that should be done by people, it only provides a help to gain some early insights and guide decisions.

In addition to sentiment analysis, other types of techniques are also available to gain a deeper understanding of text data.

4.5 Other types of text classification tools

Even though sentiment analysis provides some useful information about data collected, it can also be paired with other types of text classification tools to generate better predictions and extract more meaningful insights.

4.5.1 Intent analysis

Intent analysis, also called intent classification, goes a step further by trying to analyze and understand the user's **intention** behind a message and identify whether it relates to an opinion, news, marketing, query, complaint, suggestion, and so on. It also helps categorize customers' intents by topics such as Purchase, Downgrade, Demo request, and so on.

To do this, a model needs to be trained with existing data collected from users and labelled with the different intents we would like to use for future predictions.

It works a bit similarly to the Toxicity Classifier I talked about previously in this chapter, but instead of using labels such as "severe_toxicity" or "threat", the model would be trained with labels such as "Purchase", "Need for information", "Cancellation", and so on.

Feeding this labelled data from real customers' comments, requests, and complaints to an algorithm would allow it to find patterns of vocabulary used, semantics, arrangements of words in a sentence, used by people when expressing similar intents.

4.5.2 Named Entity Recognition

Named entity recognition (NER), also known as entity identification, entity chunking, or entity extraction, extracts entities such as people, locations, organizations, and dates from text.

For example, if we take the following sample paragraph from the Rosa Parks' Wikipedia page:

> *Rosa Louise McCauley Parks (February 4, 1913* – October 24, 2005*) was an American* activist *in the* civil rights movement *best known for her pivotal role in the* Montgomery bus boy-cott. *The* United States Congress *has called her "the first lady of civil rights" and "the mother of the freedom movement."*

> —Quote source: `https://en.wikipedia.org/wiki/Rosa_Parks`

Named entity recognition would allow us to extract and classify the following terms:

- **Person**: Rosa Louise McCauley Parks

- **Location**: Montgomery, United States

- **Date**: February 4, 1913, October 24, 2005

- **Organization**: United States Congress

NER models have a wide range of applications including automatic summarizing of resumes to aim at simplifying the recruitment process by automatically scanning a huge amount of documents and shortlist candidates based on terms found in them.

4.5.3 Text summarization

As the name indicates, text summarization is a technique usually used to create an accurate summary that captures the main pieces of information in a longer text.

These summaries allow people to navigate content more effectively by reducing reading time and helping in the selection process of research documents.

The goal of this technique is not only to capture the main words of a document and generate a shorter sentence, but also to create something that reads fluently as a new stand-alone piece of content. It should result in a summary that is as good as those a human would write.

Examples of day-to-day text summarization we are already familiar with include

- News headlines
- Notes from meetings
- Synopses
- Biographies

For automatic text summarization using machine learning, there exist two approaches: **extractive** and **abstractive.**

Extractive text summarization is the process of selecting phrases in a source document to generate a summary. It involves ranking the relevance of phrases in the source and only selecting the ones that are the most relevant to the meaning of the document.

Abstractive text summarization involves generating brand-new phrases that convey the most critical information from the source document. It uses advanced natural language processing techniques to interpret and examine the text and produce shorter sentences in a new way.

4.5.4 Question Answering with TensorFlow.js

Question Answering is a discipline within the field of natural language processing that is concerned with building systems that automatically answer questions posed by humans in a natural language.

A machine learning model takes a passage and a question as input and is able to return a segment of the passage that is likely to answer the question asked, as output.

In the next few pages, we are going to use the MobileBERT model, a lightweight version of the BERT (Bidirectional Encoder Representations from Transformers) model from Google, to build a system capable of answering questions submitted by humans based on a set of paragraphs.

Importing the model

To set up our project, we need to start by importing TensorFlow.js and the model.

Listing 4-19. Importing TensorFlow.js and the QNA model in an HTML file

```
<script src="https://cdn.jsdelivr.net/npm/@tensorflow/tfjs">
</script>
<script src="https://cdn.jsdelivr.net/npm/@tensorflow-models/
qna"></script>
```

Or

Listing 4-20. Importing TensorFlow.js and the QNA model as package in a JavaScript file

```
const qna = require('@tensorflow-models/qna');
```

If you decide to use it as a NPM module, you do not need to import the @tensorflow/tfjs library; however, you will need to make sure you have installed the peer dependencies for tfjs-core and tfjs-converter.

Loading the model

Once the model is imported, we need to load it in our application. Two options are available to do this.

First, you can load it without providing a config object.

Listing 4-21. Default way to load the model

```
const model = await qna.load();
```

This way of loading the model is the one you should probably use if you want to use Google's Question Answering model hosted on the Google Cloud Platform (GCP) provider.

If you live in an area or country that does not have access to the model hosted on GCP, you can provide a configuration object that will contain the custom URL of the model hosted on your own servers.

Listing 4-22. Loading the model using custom configurations

```
const config = { modelUrl: "https://yourown-server/qna/model.
json" };
const customModel = await qna.load(config);
```

These two ways of loading the model will return a model object that we can call methods on to predict our answers.

Predictions

Generating answers is done using the `findAnswers()` method on the model object. This method accepts two arguments: the first one is the question the user would like to ask, and the second is the associated passage that content needs to be extracted from.

Listing 4-23. Generating predictions

```
const answers = await model.findAnswers(question, passage);
```

These two parameters need to be strings.

The answers variable that will hold the results of the predictions will be an array of elements with the following shape:

```
[
  {
    text: "Angela Davis",
    startIndex: 1143,
    endIndex: 1156,
    score: 0.8380282521247864
  }
]
```

The `text` property represents the answer to the question the person would have asked. The `score` is the confidence level for the prediction. The higher it is, the more confident the model is that this answer is correct. The `startIndex` and `endIndex` represent the indices of the starting and ending character where the expression was found in the passage.

Complete example

Let's put all these code samples together, reuse one of our examples from the previous sections, and ask questions about Rosa Parks.

Listing 4-24. HTML code

```html
<html lang="en">
  <head>
    <meta charset="UTF-8" />
    <meta name="viewport" content="width=device-width, initial-
    scale=1.0" />
    <title>Question Answering</title>
  </head>
  <body>
    <script src="https://cdn.jsdelivr.net/npm/@tensorflow/
    tfjs"></script>
    <script src="https://cdn.jsdelivr.net/npm/@tensorflow-
    models/qna"></script>
    <script src="index.js"></script>
  </body>
</html>
```

Listing 4-25. JavaScript code in the index.js file

```javascript
const init = async () => {

  const passage = "Rosa Louise McCauley Parks (February 4,
  1913 - October    24, 2005) was an American activist in the
  civil rights
    movement best known for her pivotal role in the Montgomery
    bus boycott. The United States Congress has called her 'the
    first lady of civil rights' and 'the mother of the freedom
    movement'";

  const question = "When was Rosa born?";

  const model = await qna.load();
```

```
  const answers = await model.findAnswers(question, passage);

  console.log(answers);

};

init();
```

This code will log the following output in your browser's console.

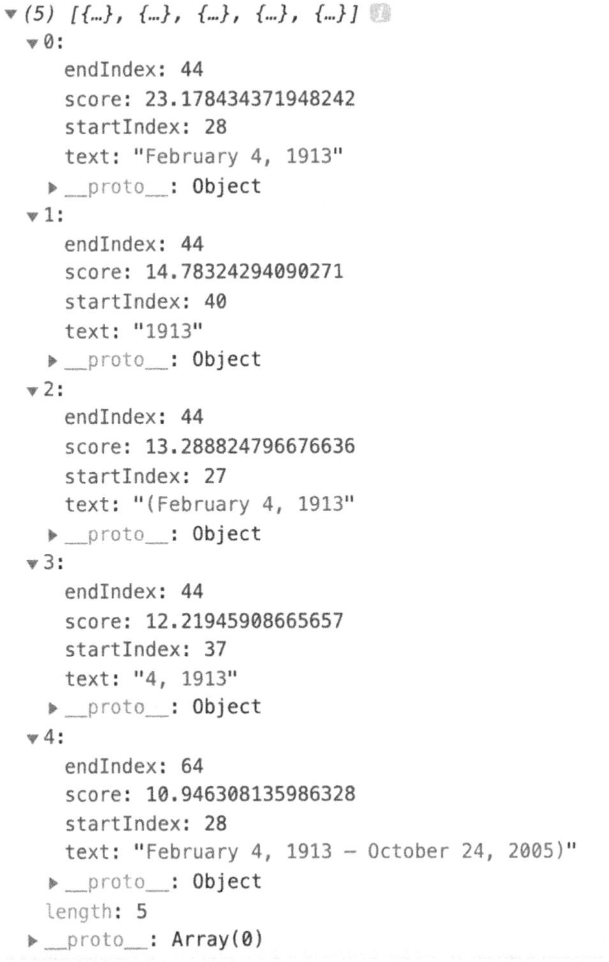

```
▼ (5) [{…}, {…}, {…}, {…}, {…}]
  ▼ 0:
      endIndex: 44
      score: 23.178434371948242
      startIndex: 28
      text: "February 4, 1913"
    ▶ __proto__: Object
  ▼ 1:
      endIndex: 44
      score: 14.78324294090271
      startIndex: 40
      text: "1913"
    ▶ __proto__: Object
  ▼ 2:
      endIndex: 44
      score: 13.288824796676636
      startIndex: 27
      text: "(February 4, 1913"
    ▶ __proto__: Object
  ▼ 3:
      endIndex: 44
      score: 12.21945908665657
      startIndex: 37
      text: "4, 1913"
    ▶ __proto__: Object
  ▼ 4:
      endIndex: 64
      score: 10.946308135986328
      startIndex: 28
      text: "February 4, 1913 – October 24, 2005)"
    ▶ __proto__: Object
    length: 5
  ▶ __proto__: Array(0)
```

Figure 4-8. *Prediction output in the browser's console to the question "When was Rosa born?"*

As we can see in the preceding screenshot, the answers come back as an array of five elements. The one with the highest score is "February 4, 1913", which is the correct answer to the question "When was Rosa born?"!

Also, if we observe the subsequent predictions, they are all somewhat correct as they contain either a part of the birth date or the birth and death dates.

We could think maybe we just got lucky on that one, so let's try another question, for example: "Who was Rosa Parks?".

When asking this question, we get the following answers.

```
▼ (2) [{…}, {…}] ▣
  ▼ 0:
      endIndex: 118
      score: 5.861338138580322
      startIndex: 69
      text: "an American activist in the civil rights movement"
    ▶ __proto__: Object
  ▼ 1:
      endIndex: 118
      score: 5.157596826553345
      startIndex: 81
      text: "activist in the civil rights movement"
    ▶ __proto__: Object
    length: 2
  ▶ __proto__: Array(0)
```

Figure 4-9. *Prediction output in the browser's console to the question "Who was Rosa Parks?"*

This time, our answers array contains only two objects. However, these predictions are correct!

An interesting aspect of this is that our question mentioned "Rosa Parks", whereas our passage mentioned her full name "Rosa Louise McCauley Parks", and the model was still able to understand who our question was about.

This is pretty impressive and has huge potential, but, as with every machine learning model, it has its limits.

For example, when changing the question to "How was Rosa Parks called?", expecting the answers "the first lady of civil rights" or "the mother of the freedom movement", the predictions array came back empty, meaning the model could not find answers to this question in the passage.

However, when modifying the question a little bit to be more precise ("What did the United States Congress call Rosa Parks?"), the model managed to provide the right answers – the first one being this.

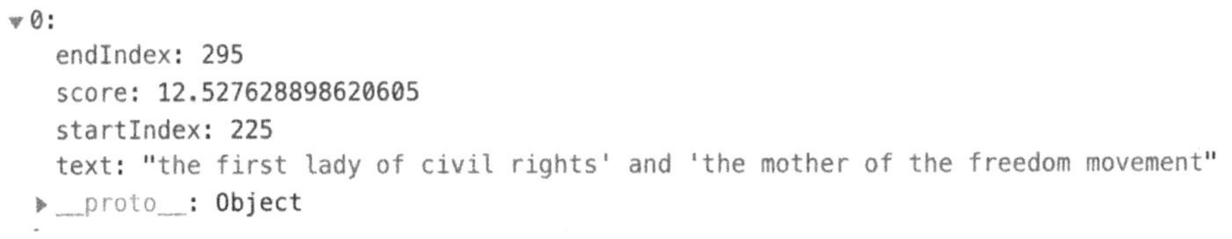

```
▼ 0:
    endIndex: 295
    score: 12.527628898620605
    startIndex: 225
    text: "the first lady of civil rights' and 'the mother of the freedom movement"
  ▶ __proto__: Object
```

Figure 4-10. *First prediction output in the browser's console to the question "What did the United States Congress call Rosa Parks?"*

Unfortunately, asking the question this way would have probably required a certain kind of knowledge from the user. A person unfamiliar with the details of Rosa Parks' life would have most likely asked the question in a similar format to "What was Rosa Parks called?", which returned no answer.

Building an interactive education tool

In the preceding code samples, we only used this model to log the results in the browser's developer tools. However, let's use this code to build an interactive education tool, in which users would be able to learn about historical figures, using Question Answering.

For this project, to make it simpler, we're going to store data about a few preselected people in our code base as JSON files. If you are not familiar with it, JSON stands for JavaScript Object Notation and refers to a file format for storing data.

If you wanted to go a step further, you could try to use the MediaWiki API to let users request for any public figure they would want and fetch data dynamically.

The following application is going to have information about three historical figures, let the user decide which one they would like to learn more about, and provide an input field to ask different questions to display the answer with the highest probability, predicted by the machine learning model.

The final state of this project is going to contain three screens and look something like this.

Figure 4-11. *Home page of the project*

Figure 4-12. *Page to select the public figure to learn more about*

Figure 4-13. *Page to ask questions and display the best answer predicted*

As you may have noticed, I kept the design very minimal because I want to focus on the functionality. The important takeaway from this project is how to create a quick user interface using the Question Answering model.

Now that you have a better idea of what we are about to build, let's dive into the different features and code samples.

Step 1: Loading page

Figure 4-14. *Home page of the project*

Loading a pre-trained machine learning model into your application will always have an impact on performance as they tend to be quite heavy. As a result, it is important to think in advance about what kind of user experience you want to create to improve the perceived performance.

This could include loading the model in the background early on, so by the time the user gets to the experience, it is loaded and ready to be used; or providing a loading animation to indicate that the user needs to wait for the interface to be usable.

The latter is not the best option as the user clearly is forced to wait before being able to interact with the experience; however, in the case of this project, this is the method we are going to use, as the only feature of the application is the interaction with the model.

To display this loading state, we have a button element in our HTML file that has a default state of disabled, to prevent the user from trying to run predictions before the model is available.

Listing 4-26. HTML code sample to show some intro text and a button with initial loading state

```
<section class="intro">
   <h1>Hidden figures</h1>
   <h3>
     Using machine learning, learn about 3 NASA engineers by
     asking questions about their lives!
   </h3>
   <button disabled>Loading...</button>
 </section>
```

Then, in the JavaScript file, we can start loading the model as soon as the page loads and change the state of the button once the model is ready.

Listing 4-27. JavaScript code sample to load the model and update the state of the button when the model is loaded

```
let model;
const loadModel = async () => await qna.load();

const init = async () => {
```

```
model = await loadModel();

const startButton = document.querySelector(".intro button");

startButton.removeAttribute("disabled");
startButton.innerHTML = "Start";
};

init();
```

The preceding code sample shows that, as soon as the `loadModel` function has finished loading the model, we remove the disabled state of the button to make it interactive and change its content to "Start" to indicate that the user can start the experience.

At this stage, once the user clicks the start button, we hide this content to show the three options available.

Step 2: Selection page

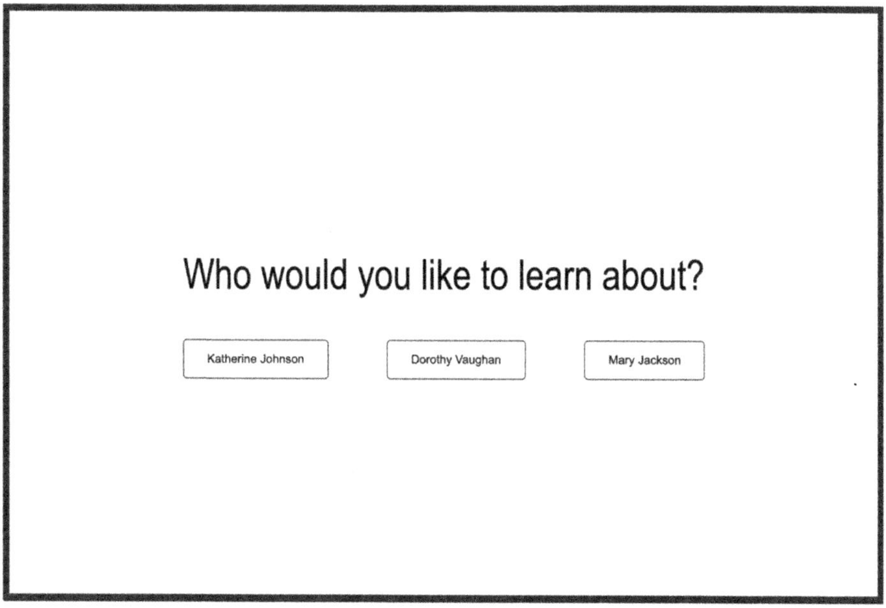

Figure 4-15. *Page to select the engineer to learn more about*

For the purpose of this small demo, I hard-coded the name of the three engineers in the button elements in the HTML file; however, if you were building something with more entries, or if they were dynamically generated, you could also replace the content of the buttons dynamically in JavaScript.

Listing 4-28. HTML code sample with buttons containing the name of the three NASA engineers

```
<section class="selection">
   <h1>Who would you like to learn about?</h1>
   <section class="buttons">
     <button class="figure">Katherine Johnson</button>
     <button class="figure">Dorothy Vaughan</button>
     <button class="figure">Mary Jackson</button>
   </section>
</section>
```

In our JavaScript file, we need to add an event listener for clicks on these buttons and fetch the JSON data.

To avoid loading all content at once, I created a JSON file for each person, so that the code is going to fetch only the data the user has asked for.

As a result, I have three JSON files that I named:

- dorothyVaughan.json

- katherineJohnsons.json

- maryJackson.json

This way, when the user clicks one of the three buttons, the following code will execute the fetching and prepare for the following prediction page.

Listing 4-29. JavaScript code to fetch data when clicking one of the buttons

```
const engineers = {
  "Katherine Johnson": "katherineJohnson",
  "Dorothy Vaughan": "dorothyVaughan",
  "Mary Jackson": "maryJackson",
};

figureButtons.forEach(button => {
  button.onclick = e => {
    const dataFile = engineers[e.target.textContent];

    fetch(`${window.location.href}${dataFile}.json`)
      .then(response => response.json())
      .then(data => {
        figureData = data;
        const label = document.getElementsByTagName("label")[0];
        label.innerHTML = `What would you like to know about
        ${e.target.textContent}?`;
      });
  };
});
```

In the preceding code sample, I started by creating an object to map the names displayed in the UI to the names of the associated JSON file.

Then, for each of the three buttons, I listen for click events, look at the content of the button clicked to get the name of the JSON file, and use the `fetch` function to get the data and store it in a `figureData` variable.

I also use the name of the person the user has chosen, to display it in the title "What would you like to know about...".

There is a bit more code related to showing and hiding HTML elements as we go through the pages, but I will share the complete code for this project at the end of this chapter.

Now that we know which person the user is interested in knowing more about, and we've fetched the related data, let's move on to the prediction page.

Step 3: Predictions

Figure 4-16. *Page to ask questions and display the best answer predicted*

Our final page has an input field, a button to run the predictions, and a paragraph that outputs the answer.

Listing 4-30. HTML code sample to display an input field and a section to display the prediction

```
<section class="question">
  <label for="question"></label>
  <input type="text" name="question" placeholder="Who was she?" />
  <button class="ask">Ask</button>
</section>

<section class="answer-block">
  <p class="input-question"></p>
  <p class="answer"></p>
</section>
```

In our JavaScript file, we need to listen to click events on the button, get the value of the input entered by the user, send it alongside the data fetched as parameters to the method to get the answers from the model, and display the first answer on the page.

The following is the code sample to do this.

Listing 4-31. JavaScript code sample to get the input string, feed it to the model, and display the output

```
const askButton = document.getElementsByClassName("ask")[0];

askButton.onclick = async () => {
  inputQuestion = document.getElementsByTagName("input")[0].value;
  const answers = await model.findAnswers(inputQuestion,
  figureData);
  displayAnswer(answers);
  document.getElementsByTagName("input")[0].value = "";
};
```

```
const displayAnswer = (answers) => {
  const inputQuestionElement = document.querySelector(
    ".answer-block .input-question"
  );
  const paragraphElement = document.
  getElementsByClassName("answer")[0];

  if (!answers[0]) {
    inputQuestionElement.innerHTML = "";
    paragraphElement.innerHTML = `Mmmm I don't seem to have the
    answer to this question 🤪`;
    return;
  }
  inputQuestionElement.innerHTML = `The answer to your question
  "${inputQuestion}" is:`;
  paragraphElement.innerHTML = `${answers[0].text}`;

  document.getElementsByClassName("answer-block")[0].style.
  display = "block";
};
```

In the first part of the preceding code, we listen to click events, get the input question, and call the findAnswers method with the question and the figureData variable we used in the previous section to store the data fetched from the JSON file.

We then call a function called displayAnswer to which we pass the answers returned by the model, to display it on the page.

As mentioned a bit earlier in this chapter, sometimes, the model is not going to find answers to a question and will return an empty array. We need to handle this case first, and here, we display a generic message.

Then, if the model has found answers, we display the first one in the array as it is the one with the highest probability to be correct.

And that's it!

In less than 100 lines of JavaScript, you can create a small interactive project allowing users to ask questions and learn about different topics using machine learning!

If you want the complete code sample for this, you can find the HTML and JavaScript in the following listing.

Listing 4-32. Complete HTML code

```
<html lang="en">
  <head>
    <meta charset="UTF-8" />
    <meta name="viewport" content="width=device-width, initial-
    scale=1.0" />
    <title>Interactive education tool</title>
    <link rel="stylesheet" href=" styles.css" />
  </head>
  <body>
    <section class="intro">
      <h1>Hidden figures</h1>
      <h3>
        Using machine learning, learn about 3 NASA engineers by
        asking questions about their lives!
      </h3>
      <button disabled>Loading...</button>
    </section>
    <main>
      <section class="selection">
        <h1>Who would you like to learn about?</h1>
        <section class="buttons">
          <button class="figure">Katherine Johnson</button>
          <button class="figure">Dorothy Vaughan</button>
```

```
      <button class="figure">Mary Jackson</button>
    </section>
  </section>

  <section class="question">
    <label for="question"></label>
    <input type="text" name="question" placeholder="Who was
    she?" />
    <button class="ask">Ask</button>
  </section>

  <section class="answer-block">
    <p class="input-question"></p>
    <p class="answer"></p>
  </section>
</main>

<script src="https://cdn.jsdelivr.net/npm/@tensorflow/
tfjs"></script>
<script src="https://cdn.jsdelivr.net/npm/@tensorflow-
models/qna"></script>
<script src="index.js"></script>
</body>
</html>
```

Listing 4-33. Example JSON data for the file katherineJohnson.json

"Dorothy Johnson Vaughan (September 20, 1910 – November 10, 2008) was an American mathematician and human computer who worked for the National Advisory Committee for Aeronautics (NACA), and NASA, at Langley Research Center in Hampton, Virginia. In 1949, she became acting supervisor of the West Area Computers, the first African-American woman to supervise a group of staff at the center. She later was promoted officially to the position. During her 28-year career, Vaughan prepared for the introduction of machine computers in the early 1960s by teaching herself and her staff the programming language of Fortran. She later headed the programming section of the Analysis and Computation Division (ACD) at Langley. Vaughan is one of the women featured in Margot Lee Shetterly's history Hidden Figures: The Story of the African-American Women Who Helped Win the Space Race (2016). It was adapted as a biographical film of the same name, also released in 2016. In 2019, Vaughan was awarded the Congressional Gold Medal posthumously."

Listing 4-34. Example JSON data for the file maryJackson.json

"Mary Jackson (née Winston, April 9, 1921 – February 11, 2005) was an American mathematician and aerospace engineer at the National Advisory Committee for Aeronautics (NACA), which in 1958 was succeeded by the National Aeronautics and Space Administration (NASA). She worked at Langley Research Center in Hampton, Virginia, for most of her career. She started as a computer at the segregated West Area Computing division in 1951. She took advanced engineering classes and, in 1958, became NASA's first black female engineer. After 34 years at NASA, Jackson had earned the most senior engineering title available. She realized she could not earn further promotions without becoming a supervisor. She accepted a demotion to become a manager of both the Federal Women's Program, in the NASA Office of Equal Opportunity Programs and of the Affirmative Action Program. In this role, she worked to influence the hiring and promotion of women in NASA's science, engineering, and mathematics careers. Jackson's story features in the 2016 non-fiction book Hidden Figures: The American Dream and the Untold Story of the Black Women Who Helped Win the Space Race. She is one of the three protagonists in Hidden Figures, the film adaptation released the same year. In 2019, Jackson was posthumously awarded the Congressional Gold Medal. In 2020 the Washington, D.C. headquarters of NASA was renamed the Mary W. Jackson NASA Headquarters."

Listing 4-35. Example JSON data for the file dorothyVaughan.json

"Dorothy Johnson Vaughan (September 20, 1910 – November 10, 2008) was an American mathematician and human computer who worked for the National Advisory Committee for Aeronautics (NACA), and NASA, at Langley Research Center in Hampton, Virginia. In 1949, she became acting supervisor of the West Area Computers, the first African-American woman to supervise a group of staff at the center. She later was promoted officially to the position. During her 28-year career, Vaughan prepared for the introduction of machine computers in the early 1960s by teaching herself and her staff the programming language of Fortran. She later headed the programming section of the Analysis and Computation Division (ACD) at Langley. Vaughan is one of the women featured in Margot Lee Shetterly's history Hidden Figures: The Story of the African-American Women Who Helped Win the Space Race (2016). It was adapted as a biographical film of the same name, also released in 2016. In 2019, Vaughan was awarded the Congressional Gold Medal posthumously."

Listing 4-36. Complete JavaScript code

```javascript
const engineers = {
  "Katherine Johnson": "katherineJohnson",
  "Dorothy Vaughan": "dorothyVaughan",
  "Mary Jackson": "maryJackson",
};

let inputQuestion;
let model;

const loadModel = async () => await qna.load();

const init = async () => {
  const startButton = document.querySelector(".intro button");
  model = await loadModel();

  startButton.removeAttribute("disabled");
  startButton.innerHTML = "Start";
  startButton.onclick = () => {
    document.getElementsByTagName("main")[0].style.display =
    "block";
    document.getElementsByClassName("intro")[0].style.display =
    "none";
  };

  const figureButtons = document.getElementsByClassName("figure");
  let figureData;

  figureButtons.forEach((button) => {
    button.onclick = (e) => {
      const dataFile = engineers[e.target.textContent];

      fetch(`${window.location.href}${dataFile}.json`)
        .then((response) => response.json())
```

```
      .then((data) => {
        document.getElementsByClassName("selection")[0].
        style.display =
           "none";
        figureData = data;
        const questionInput = document.getElementsByClassName
        ("question")[0];
        const label = document.getElementsByTagName("label")[0];
        label.innerHTML = `What would you like to know about
        ${e.target.textContent}?`;
        questionInput.style.display = "block";
      });
    };
  });

  const askButton = document.getElementsByClassName("ask")[0];

  askButton.onclick = async () => {
    inputQuestion = document.getElementsByTagName("input")[0].
    value;
    const answers = await model.findAnswers(inputQuestion,
    figureData);
    displayAnswer(answers);
    document.getElementsByTagName("input")[0].value = "";
  };
};

const displayAnswer = (answers) => {
  const inputQuestionElement = document.querySelector(
    ".answer-block .input-question"
  );
  const paragraphElement = document.
getElementsByClassName("answer")[0];
```

```
if (!answers[0]) {
  inputQuestionElement.innerHTML = "";
  paragraphElement.innerHTML = `Mmmm I don't seem to have the
  answer to this question 🥴`;
  return;
}
inputQuestionElement.innerHTML = `The answer to your question
"${inputQuestion}" is:`;
paragraphElement.innerHTML = `${answers[0].text}`;

document.getElementsByClassName("answer-block")[0].style.
display = "block";
};

init();
```

In the code samples we just went through, questions are captured in an input field that users have to type in. However, there are other ways to get the same kind of information using another Web API.

Getting input data from the Web Speech API

A way to make this project even more interactive would be to allow people to ask their questions using their own voice rather than typing on their keyboard.

The Web API that enables speech recognition is the Web Speech API. Using this API, we can add speech-to-text functionality to this project and even text-to-speech with SpeechSynthesis, if we want the answers to also be read out loud.

The amount of code needed to add this feature is relatively small. Considering we already went through the core of the application, it will only impact the part that captures user's input.

To start using the Web Speech API, you need to include the following lines in your JavaScript file.

Listing 4-37. Initial setup to use the Web Speech API

```
var SpeechRecognition = SpeechRecognition ||
webkitSpeechRecognition;
var SpeechRecognitionEvent = SpeechRecognitionEvent ||
webkitSpeechRecognitionEvent;
```

These lines will allow you to have access to the speech recognition interface.

Then, to start using this interface, you need to create a speech recognition instance using the following.

Listing 4-38. Instantiate a new SpeechRecognition instance

```
const recognition = new SpeechRecognition();
```

Before starting the recognition, you can set a few parameters on your recognition instance. Personally, I set the following ones.

Listing 4-39. Optional parameters

```
recognition.continuous = false;
recognition.lang = "en-US";
recognition.interimResults = false;
```

The first one indicates that the listening and recognition is not continuous, meaning you will need a user interaction every time you want to listen to a question from the user. Setting it to false allows you to listen only when the user means to interact with the interface, instead of listening nonstop.

The second setting is the language of the recognition for the request. If unset, it will default to use the language of the HTML document root element, defined in your `lang` attribute.

At the moment, the list of languages available to use with the SpeechRecognition API includes

```
[
  ['Afrikaans',          ['af-ZA']],
  ['አማርኛ',              ['am-ET']],
  ['Azərbaycanca',       ['az-AZ']],
  ['বাংলা',              ['bn-BD', 'বাংলাদেশে'],
                         ['bn-IN', 'ভারত']],
  ['Bahasa Indonesia',['id-ID']],
  ['Bahasa Melayu',     ['ms-MY']],
  ['Català',            ['ca-ES']],
  ['Čeština',           ['cs-CZ']],
  ['Dansk',             ['da-DK']],
  ['Deutsch',           ['de-DE']],
  ['English',           ['en-AU', 'Australia'],
                        ['en-CA', 'Canada'],
                        ['en-IN', 'India'],
                        ['en-KE', 'Kenya'],
                        ['en-TZ', 'Tanzania'],
                        ['en-GH', 'Ghana'],
                        ['en-NZ', 'New Zealand'],
                        ['en-NG', 'Nigeria'],
                        ['en-ZA', 'South Africa'],
                        ['en-PH', 'Philippines'],
                        ['en-GB', 'United Kingdom'],
                        ['en-US', 'United States']],
  ['Español',           ['es-AR', 'Argentina'],
                        ['es-BO', 'Bolivia'],
                        ['es-CL', 'Chile'],
                        ['es-CO', 'Colombia'],
                        ['es-CR', 'Costa Rica'],
                        ['es-EC', 'Ecuador'],
                        ['es-SV', 'El Salvador'],
                        ['es-ES', 'España'],
```

```
                        ['es-US', 'Estados Unidos'],
                        ['es-GT', 'Guatemala'],
                        ['es-HN', 'Honduras'],
                        ['es-MX', 'México'],
                        ['es-NI', 'Nicaragua'],
                        ['es-PA', 'Panamá'],
                        ['es-PY', 'Paraguay'],
                        ['es-PE', 'Perú'],
                        ['es-PR', 'Puerto Rico'],
                        ['es-DO', 'República Dominicana'],
                        ['es-UY', 'Uruguay'],
                        ['es-VE', 'Venezuela']],
 ['Euskara',            ['eu-ES']],
 ['Filipino',           ['fil-PH']],
 ['Français',           ['fr-FR']],
 ['Basa Jawa',          ['jv-ID']],
 ['Galego',             ['gl-ES']],
 ['ગુજરાતી',              ['gu-IN']],
 ['Hrvatski',           ['hr-HR']],
 ['IsiZulu',            ['zu-ZA']],
 ['Íslenska',           ['is-IS']],
 ['Italiano',           ['it-IT', 'Italia'],
                        ['it-CH', 'Svizzera']],
 ['ಕನ್ನಡ',                 ['kn-IN']],
 ['ភាសាខ្មែរ',             ['km-KH']],
 ['Latviešu',           ['lv-LV']],
 ['Lietuvių',           ['lt-LT']],
 ['മലയാളം',             ['ml-IN']],
 ['मराठी',               ['mr-IN']],
 ['Magyar',             ['hu-HU']],
 ['ລາວ',                 ['lo-LA']],
 ['Nederlands',         ['nl-NL']],
```

```
['नेपाली भाषा',          ['ne-NP']],
['Norsk bokmål',      ['nb-NO']],
['Polski',            ['pl-PL']],
['Português',         ['pt-BR', 'Brasil'],
                      ['pt-PT', 'Portugal']],
['Română',            ['ro-RO']],
['සිංහල',             ['si-LK']],
['Slovenščina',       ['sl-SI']],
['Basa Sunda',        ['su-ID']],
['Slovenčina',        ['sk-SK']],
['Suomi',             ['fi-FI']],
['Svenska',           ['sv-SE']],
['Kiswahili',         ['sw-TZ', 'Tanzania'],
                      ['sw-KE', 'Kenya']],
['ქართული',           ['ka-GE']],
['Հայերեն',           ['hy-AM']],
['தமிழ்',              ['ta-IN', 'இந்தியா'],
                      ['ta-SG', 'சிங்கப்பூர்'],
                      ['ta-LK', 'இலங்கை'],
                      ['ta-MY', 'மலேசியா']],
['తెలుగు',            ['te-IN']],
['Tiếng Việt',        ['vi-VN']],
['Türkçe',            ['tr-TR']],
['اردو',              ['ur-PK', 'پاکستان'],
                      ['ur-IN', 'بھارت']],
['Ελληνικά',          ['el-GR']],
['български',         ['bg-BG']],
['Русский',           ['ru-RU']],
['Српски',            ['sr-RS']],
['Українська',        ['uk-UA']],
['한국어',              ['ko-KR']],
```

```
['中文',                    ['cmn-Hans-CN', '普通话 (中国大陆)'],
                            ['cmn-Hans-HK', '普通话 (香港)'],
                            ['cmn-Hant-TW', '中文 (台灣)'],
                            ['yue-Hant-HK', '粵語 (香港)']],
['日本語',                   ['ja-JP']],
['हिन्दी',                    ['hi-IN']],
['ภาษาไทย',                ['th-TH']]
];
```

Finally, the third setting `interimResults` set to `false` indicates I am only interested in getting the last result of the recognition, and not all interim results while I am speaking.

After setting these attributes, we can start the recognition using `recognition.start()`.

If you have not enabled the microphone on the web page already, you will be prompted to do so, but otherwise, the microphone will start listening for inputs.

To have access to the results of the recognition, you need to call the `onresult` method, like this.

Listing 4-40. Getting results from the Web Speech API

```
recognition.onresult = function (event) {
   if (event.results[0][0]){
      var result = event.results[0][0].transcript;
   }
   console.log("result", result);
};
```

Calling `onresult` returns a callback with an event object of the following shape.

```
▼ SpeechRecognitionResultList {0: SpeechRecognitionResult, length: 1} 🔢
  ▼ 0: SpeechRecognitionResult
    ▼ 0: SpeechRecognitionAlternative
        confidence: 0.9332901835441589
        transcript: "who was she"
      ▶ __proto__: SpeechRecognitionAlternative
      isFinal: true
      length: 1
    ▶ __proto__: SpeechRecognitionResult
    length: 1
  ▶ __proto__: SpeechRecognitionResultList
```

Figure 4-17. *Output of calling the onresult method*

Looking at this output helps make sense of the way we are setting the result variable in the preceding code sample: event.results[0][0]. transcript.

Another useful method we can call is onspeechend.

onspeechend is triggered when speech has stopped being detected. To avoid running recognition when not needed, we can use onspeechend to stop the recognition entirely.

Listing 4-41. Code sample to stop the recognition when the API has detected that the user has stopped talking

```
recognition.onspeechend = function () {
   recognition.stop();
};
```

Put together, the code sample for speech recognition looks like this:

```
var SpeechRecognition = SpeechRecognition ||
webkitSpeechRecognition;
var SpeechRecognitionEvent =
  SpeechRecognitionEvent || webkitSpeechRecognitionEvent;

var recognition = new SpeechRecognition();
```

131

```
const startSpeechRecognition = () => {
  recognition.continuous = false;
  recognition.lang = "en-US";
  recognition.interimResults = false;

  recognition.onspeechend = () => recognition.stop();

  recognition.onresult = function (event) {
    if (event.results[0][0]) var result = event.results[0][0].
    transcript;
    console.log("result", result);
  };
  recognition.start();
};
startSpeechRecognition();
```

In only 20 lines of JavaScript, a web application can listen to a user's voice commands!

If you wanted to add this to the project we built previously, you could implement it where we added the event listener for clicks on the "ask" button.

Instead of using the input written in the input field, you could trigger the speech recognition on click, listen to the user's voice input, and feed that to the model, the same way we sent our written input string.

Imagining you already added the basic setup of the SpeechRecognition instance from the code sample just earlier, the only change you would need to do to the project code would be in the function listening for clicks on the askButton element.

Listing 4-42. User voice commands with the QNA model

```
askButton.onclick = async () => {
  recognition.start();
  recognition.onresult = async (event) => {
```

```
    if (event.results[0][0]) {
        var result = event.results[0][0].transcript;
    }
    inputQuestion = result;

    const answers = await model.findAnswers(inputQuestion,
    figureData);
    displayAnswer(answers);
    document.getElementsByTagName("input")[0].value = "";
  };
};
```

When the user clicks the button, this code starts the speech recognition and, on result, stores the final transcript in the inputQuestion variable. This variable was already sent to the findAnswers method in the original code for this project, but now it contains input from the user's speech command.

A few changes would need to be done to the UI to reflect this functionality change (e.g., the input field is not necessarily needed anymore), but overall, the change we had to make to go from a written input to a spoken one only took a few lines of code!

Finally, if you wanted to go a little step further and have the output being read out loud to the user on top of being displayed on the screen, you can do so with the following three lines.

Listing 4-43. Code sample to get the output prediction read out loud using the SpeechSynthesis Web API

```
let speechSynth = window.speechSynthesis;
var result = new SpeechSynthesisisUtterance(answers[0].text);
speechSynth.speak(result);
```

These three lines create a speechSynthesis instance, execute a speech request passing the answer from the model, and call the `speak` method to make the speech service read the information out loud.

The default voice feels pretty robotic but a few parameters can be set to change this. I will not go into details here, but feel free to look at the MDN Web Docs for the Web Speech API for more information.

One last thing to keep in mind if you want to explore this API further is that **the browser support is not at 100%**. At the moment, it seems to be well supported on Chrome and Edge, but not Safari and Firefox.

Even though it is still pretty experimental, I would encourage you to look into it if you are interested.

This chapter contained a lot of information.

We looked into the basics of natural language processing, different types of text classification tools, various applications, and also how to implement sentiment analysis, toxicity classification, and question answering using TensorFlow.js, as well as experimenting with voice commands as a way to get text data to run predictions on.

If this is the first time you are diving into machine learning, this amount of information can feel a little bit overwhelming. However, as everything new takes time to understand, feel free to take breaks and come back to this chapter later on if you want.

The following chapter will dive into using other kind of data inputs with machine learning.

CHAPTER 5

Experimenting with inputs

In the previous chapters, we looked into how to use machine learning with images and text data to do object detection and classification, as well as sentiment analysis, toxicity classification and question answering.

These are probably the most common examples of what machine learning can do. However, this list is not exhaustive and many more inputs can be used.

In this chapter, we're going to explore different kinds of input data and build a few experimental projects to understand how to use machine learning with audio and hardware data, as well as using models focused on body and movement recognition.

5.1 Audio data

When you first read the words "audio data," you might think that this section of the book is going to focus on music; however, I am going to dive into using sound more generally.

We don't really think about it often but a lot of things around us produce sounds that give us contextual information about our environment.

© Charlie Gerard 2021
C. Gerard, *Practical Machine Learning in JavaScript*,
https://doi.org/10.1007/978-1-4842-6418-8_5

For example, the sound of thunder helps you understand the weather is probably bad without you having to look out the window, or you can recognize the sound of a plane passing by before you even see it, or even hearing the sound of waves indicates you are probably close to the ocean, and so on.

Without realizing, recognizing, and understanding the meaning of these sounds impacts our daily lives and our actions. Hearing a knock on your door indicates someone is probably behind waiting for you to open it, or hearing the sound of boiling water while you are cooking suggests that it is ready for you to pour something in it.

Using sound data and machine learning could help us leverage the rich properties of sounds to recognize certain human activities and enhance current smart systems such as Siri, Alexa, and so on.

This is what is called **acoustic activity recognition**.

Considering a lot of the devices we surround ourselves with possess a microphone, there is a lot of opportunities for this technology.

Figure 5-1. *Illustration of personal devices that possess a microphone*

So far, the smart systems some of us may be using recognize words to trigger commands, but they have no understanding of what is going on around them; your phone does not know you are in the bathroom, your Alexa device does not know you might be in the kitchen, and so on. However, they could and this could be used to create more tailored and useful digital experiences.

Before we dive into the practical part of this chapter and see how to build such systems in JavaScript using TensorFlow.js, it is helpful to start by understanding the basics of what sound is, and how it is translated to data we can use in code.

5.1.1 What is sound?

Sound is the vibration of air molecules.

If you have ever turned the volume of speakers really loud, you might have noticed that they end up moving back and forth with the music. This movement pushes on air particles, changing the air pressure and creating sound waves.

The same phenomenon happens with speech. When you speak, your vocal cords vibrate, disturbing air molecules around and changing the air pressure, creating sound waves.

A way to illustrate this phenomenon is with the following image.

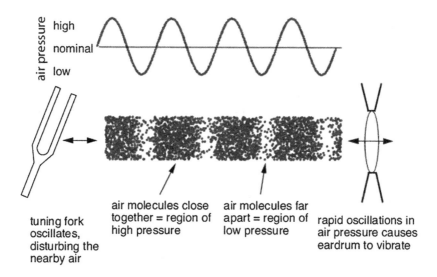

Figure 5-2. *Illustration of how sound waves work. Source: www.researchgate.net/figure/Sound-as-a-pressure-wave-The-peaks-represent-times-when-air-molecules-are-clustered_fig2_215646583*

When you hit a tuning fork, it will start vibrating. This back and forth movement will change the surrounding air pressure. The movement forward will create a higher pressure and the movement backward will create a region of lower pressure. The repetition of this movement will create waves.

On the receiver side, our eardrums vibrate with the changes of pressure and this vibration is then transformed into an electrical signal sent to the brain.

So, if sound is a change in air pressure, how do we transform a sound wave into data we can use with our devices?

To be able to interpret sound data, our devices use microphones.

There exist different types of microphones, but in general, these devices have a diaphragm or membrane that vibrates when exposed to changes of air pressure caused by sound waves.

These vibrations move a magnet near a coil inside the microphone that generate a small electrical current. Your computer then converts this signal into numbers that represent both volume and frequency.

5.1.2 Accessing audio data

In JavaScript, the Web API that lets developers access data coming from the computer's microphone is the Web Audio API.

If you have never used this API before, it's totally fine; we are going to go through the main lines you need to get set up everything.

To start, we need to access the `AudioContext` interface on the global `window` object, as well as making sure we can get permission to access an audio and video input device with `getUserMedia`.

Listing 5-1. Setup to use the Web Audio API in JavaScript

```
window.AudioContext = window.AudioContext || window.
webkitAudioContext;
navigator.getUserMedia = navigator.getUserMedia || navigator.
webkitGetUserMedia;
```

This code sample takes into consideration cross-browser compatibility.

Then, to start listening to input coming from the microphone, we need to wait for a user action on the page, for example, a click.

Once the user has interacted with the web page, we can instantiate an audio context, allow access to the computer's audio input device, and use some of the Web Audio API built-in methods to create a source and an analyzer and connect the two together to start getting some data.

Listing 5-2. JavaScript code sample to set up the audio context on click

```
document.body.onclick = async () => {
  const audioctx = new window.AudioContext();
  const stream = await navigator.mediaDevices.getUserMedia({
  audio: true });

  const source = audioctx.createMediaStreamSource(stream);
  analyser = audioctx.createAnalyser();
  analyser.smoothingTimeConstant = 0;

  source.connect(analyser);
  analyser.fftSize = 1024;
  getAudioData();
};
```

In the preceding code sample, we are using `navigator.mediaDevices.getUserMedia` to get access to the microphone. If you have ever built applications that were using audio or video input devices before, you might be familiar with writing `navigator.getUserMedia()`; however, this is deprecated and you should now be using `navigator.mediaDevices.getUserMedia()`.

Writing it the old way will still work but is not recommended as it will probably not be supported in the next few years.

Once the basic setup is done, the getAudioData function filters the raw data coming from the device to only get the frequency data.

Listing 5-3. Function to filter through the raw data to get the frequency data we will use

```
const getAudioData = () => {
  const freqdata = new Uint8Array(analyser.frequencyBinCount);
  analyser.getByteFrequencyData(freqdata);

  console.log(freqdata);

  requestAnimationFrame(getAudioData);
};
```

We also call requestAnimationFrame to continuously call this function and update the data we are logging with live data.

Altogether, you can access live data from the microphone in less than 25 lines of JavaScript!

Listing 5-4. Complete code sample to get input data from the microphone in JavaScript

```
window.AudioContext = window.AudioContext || window.
webkitAudioContext;
navigator.getUserMedia = navigator.getUserMedia || navigator.
webkitGetUserMedia;
let analyser;
```

```
document.body.onclick = async () => {
  const audioctx = new window.AudioContext();
  const stream = await navigator.mediaDevices.getUserMedia({
  audio: true });
  const source = audioctx.createMediaStreamSource(stream);
  analyser = audioctx.createAnalyser();
  analyser.smoothingTimeConstant = 0;

  source.connect(analyser);
  analyser.fftSize = 1024;
  getAudioData();
};

const getAudioData = () => {
  const freqdata = new Uint8Array(analyser.frequencyBinCount);
  analyser.getByteFrequencyData(freqdata);

  console.log(freqdata);

  requestAnimationFrame(getAudioData);
};
```

The output from this code is an array of raw data we are logging in the browser's console.

index.js:21
Uint8Array(512) [83, 128, 174, 238, 255, 255, 215, 225, 255, 255, 239,
217, 255, 255, 255, 211, 214, 232, 213, 138, 177, 207, 205, 168, 135, 1
59, 164, 139, 119, 184, 204, 194, 171, 176, 217, 218, 187, 160, 177, 17
9, 154, 109, 169, 179, 152, 105, 133, 162, 157, 131, 124, 123, 96, 93,
137, 156, 155, 143, 145, 188, 189, 149, 122, 143, 152, 130, 89, 127, 13
8, 122, 84, 79, 126, 130, 104, 45, 130, 142, 120, 8, 89, 112, 100, 67,
142, 172, 171, 138, 129, 154, 159, 138, 117, 108, 134, 127, 101, 121, 1
52, 141, …]

index.js:21
Uint8Array(512) [89, 100, 157, 230, 255, 250, 204, 212, 250, 254, 223,
216, 255, 255, 255, 217, 235, 255, 255, 215, 181, 217, 215, 178, 90, 14
7, 159, 132, 86, 164, 185, 172, 126, 195, 228, 225, 174, 172, 218, 229,
206, 167, 194, 206, 191, 148, 158, 188, 180, 129, 109, 152, 154, 134, 1
46, 196, 206, 185, 113, 175, 198, 188, 163, 164, 191, 190, 159, 134, 16
0, 161, 130, 0, 121, 144, 133, 94, 137, 157, 147, 110, 112, 148, 152, 1
30, 142, 181, 188, 168, 120, 192, 208, 198, 154, 161, 181, 175, 126, 15
2, 180, 182, …]

index.js:21
Uint8Array(512) [29, 68, 152, 234, 255, 255, 211, 218, 255, 255, 227, 2
25, 255, 255, 255, 169, 255, 255, 255, 222, 188, 222, 222, 186, 147, 15
9, 166, 147, 125, 168, 187, 175, 157, 208, 237, 234, 192, 203, 239, 24
5, 219, 178, 202, 215, 199, 141, 158, 193, 189, 153, 143, 172, 173, 13
9, 153, 199, 211, 191, 153, 180, 199, 182, 148, 179, 205, 207, 176, 15
9, 171, 174, 152, 112, 130, 146, 134, 114, 148, 172, 170, 134, 113, 15
4, 162, 143, 135, 173, 187, 164, 143, 187, 208, 201, 159, 158, 189, 19
0, 157, 139, 179, 191, …]

index.js:21
Uint8Array(512) [124, 97, 167, 236, 255, 254, 211, 219, 255, 255, 224,
227, 255, 255, 255, 204, 255, 255, 255, 224, 191, 225, 222, 182, 130, 1
65, 171, 142, 132, 177, 189, 170, 154, 215, 240, 233, 193, 204, 243, 24
3, 208, 166, 211, 223, 206, 168, 179, 195, 176, 72, 154, 184, 184, 154,
155, 196, 199, 156, 118, 191, 209, 199, 176, 187, 204, 193, 127, 148, 1
68, 168, 139, 125, 147, 147, 111, 84, 156, 179, 173, 144, 145, 164, 15
5, 124, 161, 195, 197, 171, 167, 202, 213, 192, 137, 175, 197, 190, 15
9, 166, 193, 191, …]

index.js:21
Uint8Array(512) [135, 131, 162, 233, 255, 251, 208, 216, 253, 253, 220,
224, 255, 255, 254, 219, 255, 255, 255, 213, 200, 229, 224, 189, 151, 1
73, 171, 106, 157, 187, 192, 168, 144, 216, 232, 209, 193, 213, 243, 23
6, 201, 182, 211, 207, 153, 173, 188, 195, 171, 109, 153, 170, 139, 12
5, 165, 195, 191, 172, 164, 192, 190, 113, 157, 200, 211, 192, 151, 17
0, 186, 170, 111, 123, 145, 135, 89, 129, 156, 150, 84, 115, 155, 164,
146, 131, 183, 199, 185, 150, 178, 203, 196, 160, 167, 193, 192, 157, 1
28, 179, 188, 166, …]

index.js:21
Uint8Array(512) [33, 100, 164, 230, 254, 246, 200, 211, 248, 249, 218,
214, 255, 255, 251, 224, 255, 255, 255, 206, 197, 225, 220, 185, 93, 16
1, 169, 141, 119, 182, 194, 175, 159, 212, 230, 216, 172, 193, 229, 22
4, 181, 165, 206, 210, 187, 146, 175, 192, 172, 105, 141, 162, 150, 11
1, 169, 201, 197, 162, 124, 175, 186, 174, 166, 199, 208, 183, 133, 15
7, 170, 158, 122, 79, 140, 140, 106, 89, 141, 151, 137, 118, 141, 157,
140, 102, 161, 183, 175, 158, 167, 197, 195, 162, 97, 179, 186, 162, 12
8, 163, 179, 168, …]

index.js:21
Uint8Array(512) [26, 92, 152, 223, 249, 242, 200, 207, 243, 244, 213, 2
04, 255, 255, 248, 199, 253, 255, 255, 209, 161, 212, 212, 178, 112, 14
8, 160, 141, 105, 168, 184, 169, 99, 199, 225, 221, 202, 196, 223, 222,
188, 156, 198, 205, 181, 142, 145, 175, 161, 117, 128, 152, 151, 136, 1
44, 191, 192, 165, 135, 163, 177, 168, 168, 199, 209, 193, 157, 130, 16
1, 157, 124, 57, 120, 125, 103, 90, 139, 150, 131, 72, 124, 150, 143, 1
23, 71, 157, 163, 143, 136, 186, 192, 175, 144, 143, 171, 160, 126, 13
4, 167, 164, …]

index.js:21
Uint8Array(512) [43, 77, 145, 222, 249, 242, 199, 204, 242, 244, 212, 2
06, 255, 255, 248, 164, 248, 255, 255, 206, 176, 211, 210, 180, 146, 15
2, 154, 127, 108, 161, 180, 165, 107, 194, 222, 215, 169, 167, 208, 21
2, 182, 152, 193, 205, 183, 94, 129, 165, 158, 111, 121, 154, 153, 115,
139, 181, 190, 168, 146, 176, 190, 177, 126, 170, 190, 180, 134, 133, 1
60, 163, 136, 77, 106, 125, 110, 86, 137, 156, 141, 83, 101, 128, 123,
81, 112, 152, 156, 129, 114, 173, 189, 175, 115, 126, 149, 145, 114, 11
4, 160, 166, …]

Figure 5-3. *Screenshot of the data returned by the preceding code
sample*

These arrays represent the frequencies that make up the sounds recorded by the computer's microphone. The default sample rate is 44,100Hz, which means we get about 44,000 samples of data per second.

In the format shown earlier (arrays of integers), finding patterns to recognize some type of activity seems pretty difficult. We wouldn't really be able to identify the difference between speaking, laughing, music playing, and so on.

To help make sense of this raw frequency data, we can turn it into visualizations.

5.1.3 Visualizing audio data

There are different ways to visualize sound. A couple of ways you might be familiar with are waveforms or frequency charts.

Waveform visualizers represent the displacement of sound waves over time.

Figure 5-4. *Illustration of a waveform visualization. Source: https://css-tricks.com/making-an-audio-waveform-visualizer-with-vanilla-javascript/*

On the x axis (the horizontal one) is the unit of time and on the y axis (vertical one) is the frequencies. Sound happens over a certain period of time and is made of multiple frequencies.

This way of visualizing sound is a bit too minimal to be able to identify patterns. As you can see in the illustration earlier, all frequencies that make up a sound are reduced to a single line.

Frequency charts are visualizations that represent a measure of how many times a waveform repeats in a given amount of time.

Figure 5-5. *Illustration of a frequency chart visualization*

You might be familiar with this type of audio visualization as they are probably the most common one.

This way of visualizing can maybe give you some insights about a beat as it represents repetitions or maybe about how loud the sound is as the y axis shows the volume, but that's about it.

This visualization does not give us enough information to be able to recognize and classify sounds we are visualizing.

Another type of visualization that is much more helpful is called a **spectrogram**.

A spectrogram is like a picture of a sound. It shows the frequencies that make up the sound from low to high and how they change over time. It is a visual representation of the spectrum of frequencies of a signal, a bit like a heat map of sound.

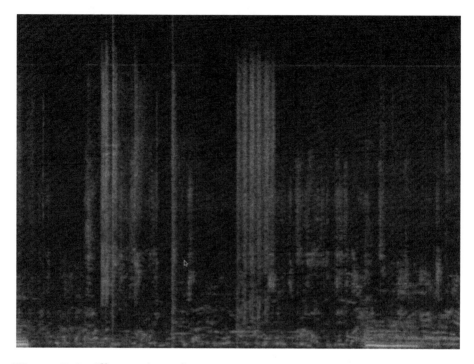

Figure 5-6. *Illustration of a spectrogram*

On the y axis is the spectrum of frequencies and, on the x axis, the amount of time. The axes seem similar to the two other type of visualizations we mentioned previously, but instead of representing all frequencies in a single line, we represent the whole spectrum.

In a spectrogram, a third axis can be helpful too, the **amplitude**. The amplitude of a sound can be described as the volume. The brighter the color, the louder the sound.

Visualizing sounds as spectrograms is much more helpful in finding patterns that would help us recognize and classify sounds.

For example, next is a screenshot of the output of a spectrogram running while I am speaking.

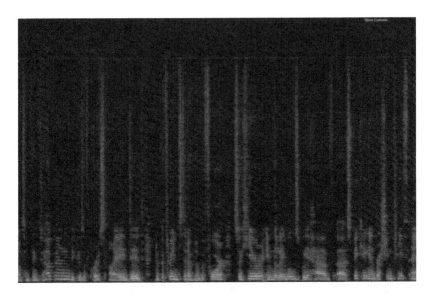

Figure 5-7. *Illustration of a spectrogram taken while speaking*

By itself, this might not help you understand why spectrograms are more helpful visualizations. The following is another screenshot of a spectrogram taken while I was clapping my hands three times.

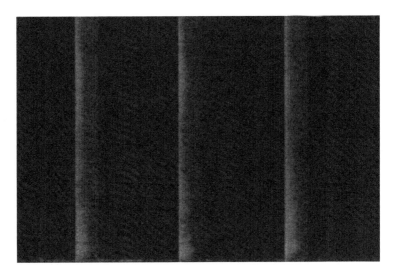

Figure 5-8. *Illustration of a spectrogram taken while clapping my hands three times*

Hopefully, it starts to make more sense! If you compare both spectrograms, you can clearly distinguish between the two activities: speaking and clapping my hands.

If you wanted, you could try to visualize more sounds like coughing, your phone ringing, toilets flushing, and so on.

Overall, the main takeaway is that spectrograms help us see the signature of various sounds more clearly and distinguish them between different activities.

If we can make this differentiation by looking at a screenshot of a spectrogram, we can hope that using this data with a machine learning algorithm will also work in finding patterns and classify this sounds to build an activity classifier.

A broader example of using spectrograms for activity classification is from a research paper published by the Carnegie Mellon University in the United States. In their paper titled "Ubicoustics: Plug-and-Play Acoustic Activity Recognition," they created spectrograms for various activities from using a chainsaw, to a vehicle driving nearby.

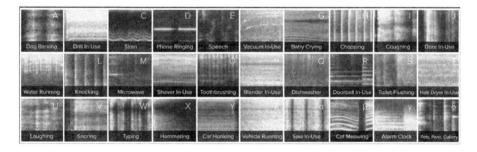

Figure 5-9. *Spectrograms collected from the research by the Carnegie Mellon University. Source:* `http://www.gierad.com/projects/ubicoustics/`

So, before we dive into using sound with machine learning, let's go through how we can turn the live data from the microphone that we logged in the console using the Web Audio API to a spectrogram.

Creating a spectrogram

In the code sample we wrote earlier, we created a getAudioData function that was getting the frequency data from the raw data and was logging it to the browser's console.

Listing 5-5. getAudioData function to get frequency data from raw data

```
const getAudioData = () => {
  const freqdata = new Uint8Array(analyser.frequencyBinCount);
  analyser.getByteFrequencyData(freqdata);

  console.log(freqdata);

  requestAnimationFrame(getAudioData);
};
```

Where we wrote our console.log statement, we are going to add the code to create the visualization.

To do this, we are going to use the Canvas API, so we need to start by adding a canvas element to our HTML file like so.

Listing 5-6. Adding a canvas element to the HTML file

```
<canvas id="canvas"></canvas>
```

In our JavaScript, we are going to be able to access this element and use some methods from the Canvas API to draw our visualization.

Listing 5-7. Getting the canvas element and context in JavaScript

```
var canvas = document.getElementById("canvas");
var ctx = canvas.getContext("2d");
```

The main concept of this visualization is to draw the spectrum of frequencies as they vary with time, so we need to get the current canvas and redraw over it every time we get new live data.

Listing 5-8. Getting the image data from the canvas element and redrawing over it

```
imagedata = ctx.getImageData(1, 0, canvas.width - 1, canvas.height);
ctx.putImageData(imagedata, 0, 0);
```

Then, we need to loop through the frequency data we get from the Web Audio API and draw them onto the canvas.

Listing 5-9. Looping through frequency data and drawing it onto the canvas

```
for (var i = 0; i < freqdata.length; i++) {
  let value = (2 * freqdata[i]) / 255;

  ctx.beginPath();
  ctx.strokeStyle = `rgba(${Math.max(0, 255 * value)},
  ${Math.max(
      0,
      255 * (value - 1)
    )}, 54, 255)`;
  ctx.moveTo(canvas.width - 1, canvas.height - i *
  (canvas.height / freqdata.length));

    ctx.lineTo(
      canvas.width - 1,
      canvas.height -
```

```
        (i * (canvas.height / freqdata.length) +
          canvas.height / freqdata.length)
  );
  ctx.stroke();
}
```

Inside this for loop, we use the beginPath method to indicate that we are going to start drawing something onto the canvas.

Then, we call strokeStyle and pass it a dynamic value that will represent the colors used to display the amplitude of the sound.

After that, we call moveTo to move the visualization 1 pixel to the left and leave space for the new input to be drawn onto the screen at the far right, drawn with lineTo.

Finally, we call the stroke method to draw the line.

Altogether, our getAudioData function should look something like this.

Listing 5-10. Full getAudioData function

```
const getAudioData = () => {
  freqdata = new Uint8Array(analyser.frequencyBinCount);
  analyser.getByteFrequencyData(freqdata);
  console.log(freqdata);
  imagedata = ctx.getImageData(1, 0, canvas.width - 1,
  canvas.height);
  ctx.putImageData(imagedata, 0, 0);

  for (var i = 0; i < freqdata.length; i++) {
    let value = (2 * freqdata[i]) / 255;

    ctx.beginPath();
    ctx.strokeStyle = `rgba(${Math.max(0, 255 * value)},
    ${Math.max(
      0,
```

```
      255 * (value - 1)
    )}, 54, 255)`;
    ctx.moveTo(
      canvas.width - 1,
      canvas.height - i * (canvas.height / freqdata.length)
    );
    ctx.lineTo(
      canvas.width - 1,
      canvas.height -
        (i * (canvas.height / freqdata.length) +
          canvas.height / freqdata.length)
    );
    ctx.stroke();
  }

  requestAnimationFrame(getAudioData);
};
```

You might be wondering why it is important to understand how to create spectrograms. The main reason is that it is what is used as training data for the machine learning algorithm.

Instead of using the raw data the way we logged it in the browser's console, we instead use pictures of spectrograms generated to transform a sound problem into an image one.

Advancements in image recognition and classification have been really good over the past few years, and algorithms used with image data have been proven to be very performant.

Also, turning sound data into an image means that we can deal with a smaller amount of data to train a model, which would result in a shorter amount of time needed.

Indeed, the default sample rate of the Web Audio API is 44KHz, which means that it collects 44,000 samples of data per second.

If we record 2 seconds of audio, it is 88,000 points of data for a single sample.

151

You can imagine that as we need to record a lot more samples, it would end up being a very large amount of data being fed to a machine learning algorithm, which would take a long time to train.

On the other hand, a spectrogram being extracted as a picture can be easily resized to a smaller size, which could end up being only a 28x28 pixel image, for example, which would result in 784 data points for a 2-second audio clip.

Now that we covered how to access live data from the microphone in JavaScript and how to transform it into a spectrogram visualization, allowing us to see how different sounds create visually different patterns, let's look into how to train a machine learning model to create a classifier.

5.1.4 Training the classifier

Instead of creating a custom machine learning algorithm for this, we are going to use instead one of the Teachable Machine experiments dedicated to sound data. You can find it at `https://teachablemachine.withgoogle.com/train/audio`.

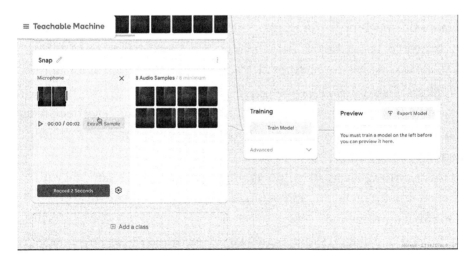

Figure 5-10. *Teachable Machine interface*

This project allows us to record samples of sound data, label them, train a machine learning algorithm, test the output, and export the model all within a single interface and in the browser!

To start, we need to record some background noise for 20 seconds using the section highlighted in red in the following figure.

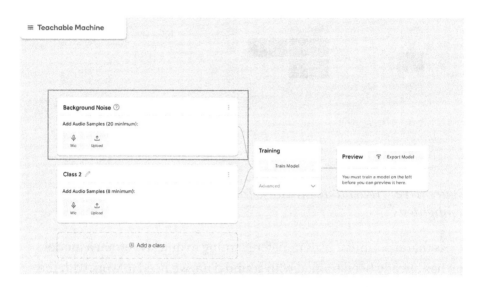

Figure 5-11. *Teachable Machine interface with background noise section highlighted*

Then, we can start to record some samples for whatever sound we would like the model to recognize later on.

The minimum amount of samples is 8 and each of them needs to be 2 seconds long.

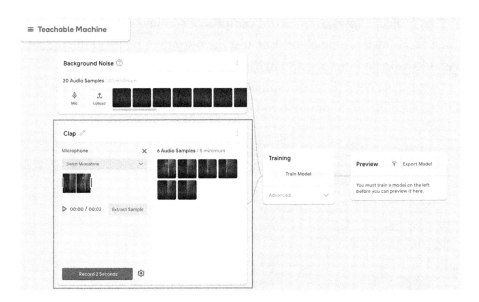

Figure 5-12. _Teachable Machine interface with custom section_
highlighted

As this experiment uses transfer learning to quickly retrain a model
that has already been trained with sound data, we need to work with the
same format the original model was trained with.

Eight samples is the minimum but you can record more if you'd like.
The more samples, the better. However, don't forget that it will also impact
the amount of time the training will take.

Once you have recorded your samples and labelled them, you can start
the live training in the browser and make sure not to close the browser
window.

Figure 5-13. *Teachable Machine interface – training the model*

When this step is done, you should be able to see some live predictions in the last step of the experiment. Before you export the model, you can try to repeat the sounds you recorded to verify the accuracy of the predictions. If you don't find it accurate enough, you can record more samples and restart the training.

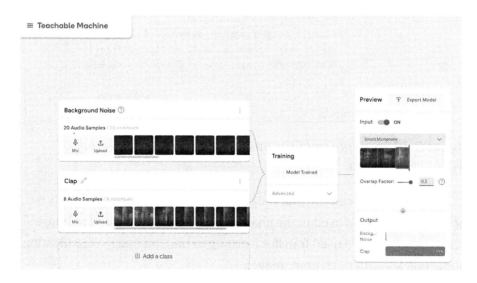

Figure 5-14. *Teachable Machine interface – running live predictions*

If you are ready to move on, you can either upload your model to some Google servers and be provided with a link to it, or download the machine learning model that was created.

If you'd like to get a better understanding of how it works in the background, how the machine learning model is created, and so on, I'd recommend having a look at the source code available on GitHub!

Even though I really like interfaces like Teachable Machine as they allow anyone to get started and experiment quickly, looking at the source code can reveal some important details. For example, the next image is how I realized that this project was using transfer learning.

While going through the code to see how the machine learning model was created and how the training was done, I noticed the following sample of code.

```
789          const finalSpectrogram: SpectrogramData = {
790            data: normalized,
791            frameSize: this.nonBatchInputShape[1]
792          };
793          this.dataset.addExample({
794            label: word,
795            spectrogram: finalSpectrogram,
796            rawAudio: options.includeRawAudio ? {
797              data: await timeData.data() as Float32Array,
798              sampleRateHz: this.audioDataExtractor.sampleRateHz
799            } :
800                                          undefined
801          });
```

Figure 5-15. *Sample from the open source GitHub repository of Teachable Machine*

On line 793, we can see that the method `addExample` is called. This is the same method we used in the chapter of this book dedicated to image recognition when we used transfer learning to train an image classification model quickly with new input images.

Noticing these details is important if you decide to experiment with re-creating this model on your own, without going through the Teachable Machine interface.

Now that we went through the training process, we can write the code to generate the predictions.

5.1.5 Predictions

Before we can start writing this code, we need to import TensorFlow.js and the speech commands model.

Listing 5-11. Import TensorFlow.js and the speech commands model in an HTML file

```
<script src="https://cdn.jsdelivr.net/npm/@tensorflow/
tfjs@1.3.1/dist/tf.min.js"></script>
<script src="https://cdn.jsdelivr.net/npm/@tensorflow-models/
speech-commands@0.4.0/dist/speech-commands.min.js"></script>
```

As I mentioned earlier, this experiment uses transfer learning, so we need to import the speech commands model that has already been trained with audio data to make it simpler and faster to get started.

The speech commands model was originally trained to recognize and classify spoken words, like "yes", "no", "up", and "down". However, here, we are using it with sounds produced by activities, so it might not be as accurate as if we were using spoken words in our samples.

Before going through the rest of the code samples, make sure you have downloaded your trained model from the Teachable Machine platform, unzipped it, and added it to your application folder.

The following code samples will assume that your model is stored in a folder called activities-model at the root of your application.

Overall, your file structure should look something like this:

- activities-model/
  - metadata.json
  - model.json
  - weights.bin
- index.html
- index.js

In our JavaScript file, we will need to create a function to load our model and start the live predictions, but before, we can create two variables to hold the paths to our model and metadata files.

Listing 5-12. Variables to refer to the model and its metadata

```
let URL = "http://localhost:8000/activities-model/";
const modelURL = `${URL}/model.json`;
const metadataURL = `${URL}metadata.json`;
```

You may have noticed that I used `localhost:8000` in the preceding code; however, feel free to change the port and make sure to update this if you decide to release your application to production.

Then, we need to load the model and ensure it is loaded before we continue.

Listing 5-13. Loading the model

```
const model = window.speechCommands.create(
    "BROWSER_FFT",
    undefined,
    modelURL,
    metadataURL
);
await model.ensureModelLoaded();
```

Once the model is ready, we can run live predictions by calling the listen method on the model.

Listing 5-14. Live predictions

```
model.listen(
    (prediction) => {
      predictionCallback(prediction.scores);
    },
    modelParameters
  );
```

Altogether, the setupModel function should look like this.

Listing 5-15. Full code sample

```
async function setupModel(URL, predictionCB) {
  predictionCallback = predictionCB;
  const modelURL = `${URL}/model.json`;
  const metadataURL = `${URL}metadata.json`;

  model = window.speechCommands.create(
    "BROWSER_FFT",
    undefined,
    modelURL,
    metadataURL
  );
  await model.ensureModelLoaded();

  const modelParameters = {
    invokeCallbackOnNoiseAndUnknown: true, // run even when
                                           //    only background
                                           //    noise is detected
    includeSpectrogram: true,
    overlapFactor: 0.5, // how often per second to sample
                        //    audio, 0.5 means twice per second
  };
```

```
model.listen(
  (prediction) => {
    predictionCallback(prediction.scores);
  },
  modelParameters
);
}
```

When called, this function will contain the predictions data in the callback invoked every time the model has a prediction.

Listing 5-16. Calling the function

```
document.body.onclick = () => {
  setupModel(URL, (data) => {
    console.log(data)
  });
}
```

```
                                                      index.js:31
▸ Float32Array(6) [0.257201224565506, 0.03705264627933502, 0.0833798721432685
  9, 0.298702597618103, 0.005999754182994366, 0.31766390800476074]
                                                      index.js:31
▸ Float32Array(6) [0.03475930541753769, 0.006106598302721977, 0.0462522730231
  2851, 0.13669534027576447, 0.011434062384068966, 0.7647523283958435]
                                                      index.js:31
▸ Float32Array(6) [0.053720273077487946, 0.005865324754267931, 0.000886341556
  9067001, 0.09962046891450882, 0.08540159463882446, 0.7545061707496643]
                                                      index.js:31
▸ Float32Array(6) [0.3078163266181946, 0.06562558561563492, 0.055476136505603
  79, 0.008057372644543648, 0.1327144801616687, 0.43031013011932373]
                                                      index.js:31
▸ Float32Array(6) [0.3559364676475525, 0.042778950184583664, 0.14965918660163
  88, 0.07153713703155518, 0.011761280708014965, 0.3683270215988159]
                                                      index.js:31
▸ Float32Array(6) [0.14595471322536469, 0.007608985062688589, 0.1830988824367
  5232, 0.09879795461893082, 0.07478856295347214, 0.4897507429122925]
                                                      index.js:31
▸ Float32Array(6) [0.0569005310535309, 0.20347410440444946, 0.01589132286608
  219, 0.03282298892736435, 0.006698716897517443, 0.6842125058174133]
                                                      index.js:31
▸ Float32Array(6) [0.0013897910248488188, 0.022207483649253845, 0.00415220065
  0423765, 0.7639986276626587, 0.001311262953095138, 0.2069406509399414]
                                                      index.js:31
▸ Float32Array(6) [0.021098019555211067, 0.008434894494712353, 0.010173309594
  392776, 0.9487842321395874, 0.008170297369360924, 0.0033943753503263]
                                                      index.js:31
▸ Float32Array(6) [0.0013747347984462976, 0.008676007390022278, 0.00014024447
  59150967, 0.06211625412106514, 0.00014554218796547502, 0.92754727602005]
                                                      index.js:31
▸ Float32Array(6) [0.00005835531555931084, 0.00008532476931577548, 0.00959081
  5752744675, 0.26799315214157104, 0.34995806217193604, 0.3723142445087433]
                                                      index.js:31
▸ Float32Array(6) [0.07940792292356491, 0.11387252807617188, 0.03461777791380
  882, 0.45582231879234314, 0.013467184267938137, 0.30281224846839905]
                                                      index.js:31
▸ Float32Array(6) [0.01299488265067339, 0.010118764825165272, 0.0289990883320
  57, 0.3586713671684265, 0.0200209878385067, 0.5691949129104614]
                                                      index.js:31
▸ Float32Array(6) [0.7709361910820007, 0.01564336009323597, 0.004517614375799
  894, 0.0090259974822402, 0.0037714627105742693, 0.19610533118247986]
                                                      index.js:31
▸ Float32Array(6) [0.7445350885391235, 0.0002750786079559475, 0.0006227701669
  558883, 0.0008174973190762103, 0.00045162977767176926, 0.25329774618148804]
                                                      index.js:31
▸ Float32Array(6) [0.27034103870391846, 0.11694413423538208, 0.03831345215439
  7964, 0.149861142039299, 0.11516861617565155, 0.3093716502189636]
                                                      index.js:31
▸ Float32Array(6) [0.0619678907096385, 0.25936102867126465, 0.0370093174278
  7361, 0.2021610587835312, 0.007632546126842499, 0.4318680167198181]
                                                      index.js:31
▸ Float32Array(6) [0.09623850882053375, 0.47506967186927795, 0.04847054556012
  1536, 0.210972860455513, 0.00822751596570015, 0.161020889878273]
```

Figure 5-16. *Example of data returned when calling the function*

This array containing the results of the prediction is ordered by label used. In the previous example, I had trained the model with six different labels so each array returned contained six values.

In each array, the value closest to 1 represents the label predicted.

To match the data predicted with the correct label, we can create an array containing the labels we used for training and use it when calling the setupModel function.

Listing 5-17. Mapping scores to labels

```
const labels = [
  "Coughing",
  "Phone ringing",
  "Speaking",
  "_background_noise_",
];
let currentPrediction;

document.body.onclick = () => {
  setupModel(URL, (data) => {
    let maximum = Math.max(...data);
    if (maximum > 0.7) {
      let maxIndex = data.indexOf(maximum);
      currentPrediction = labels[maxIndex];
      console.log(currentPrediction);
    }
  });
}
```

In less than 100 lines of JavaScript, we are able to load and run a machine learning model that can classify live audio input!

Listing 5-18. Full code sample

```
let model, predictionCallback;
let URL = "http://localhost:8000/activities-model/";

const labels = [
  "Coughing",
  "Phone ringing",
  "Speaking",
  "_background_noise_",
];

let currentPrediction, previousPrediction;
currentPrediction = previousPrediction;

document.body.onclick = () => {
  setupModel(URL, (data) => {
    let maximum = Math.max(...data);
    if (maximum > 0.7) {
      let maxIndex = data.indexOf(maximum);
      currentPrediction = labels[maxIndex];
      console.log(currentPrediction);
    }
  });
};

async function setupModel(URL, predictionCB) {
  const modelURL = `${URL}/model.json`;
  const metadataURL = `${URL}metadata.json`;

  model = window.speechCommands.create(
    "BROWSER_FFT",
    undefined,
    modelURL,
```

```
    metadataURL
  );
  await model.ensureModelLoaded();

  // This tells the model how to run when listening for audio
  const modelParameters = {
    invokeCallbackOnNoiseAndUnknown: true, // run even when
                                        only background
                                        noise is detected
    includeSpectrogram: true, // give us access to numerical
                          audio data
    overlapFactor: 0.5, // how often per second to sample
                      audio, 0.5 means twice per second
  };

  model.listen(
    (prediction) => {
      predictionCallback(prediction.scores);
    },
    modelParameters
  );
}
```

5.1.6 Transfer learning API

In the previous section, we covered how to record sound samples and train the model using the Teachable Machine experiment, for simplicity. However, if you are looking to implement this in your own application and let users run this same process themselves, you can use the transfer learning API.

This API lets you build your own interface and call API endpoints to record samples, train the model, and run live predictions.

Recording samples

Let's imagine a very simple web interface with a few buttons.

Figure 5-17. *Web interface with a few button elements*

Some of these buttons are used to collect sample data, one button to start the training and the last one to trigger the live predictions.

To get started, we need an HTML file with these six buttons and two script tags to import TensorFlow.js and the Speech Commands model.

Listing 5-19. HTML file

```html
<html lang="en">
  <head>
    <title>Speech recognition</title>
    <script src="https://cdn.jsdelivr.net/npm/@tensorflow/
    tfjs@1.3.1/dist/tf.min.js"></script>
    <script src="https://cdn.jsdelivr.net/npm/@tensorflow-
    models/speech-commands@0.4.0/dist/speech-commands.min.js">
    </script>
  </head>
  <body>
    <section>
        <button id="red">Red</button>
        <button id="blue">Blue</button>
        <button id="green">Green</button>
        <button id="background">Background</button>
        <button id="train">Train</button>
        <button id="predict">Predict</button>
    </section>
```

```
    <script src="index.js"></script>
  </body>
</html>
```

In the JavaScript file, before being able to run these actions, we need to create the model, ensure it is loaded, and pass a main label to our model to create a collection that will contain our audio samples.

Listing 5-20. Set up the recognizers

```
const init = async () => {
  const baseRecognizer = speechCommands.create("BROWSER_FFT");
  await baseRecognizer.ensureModelLoaded();
  transferRecognizer = baseRecognizer.createTransfer("colors");
};
```

Then, we can add event listeners on our buttons so they will collect samples on click. For this, we need to call the collectExample method on our recognizer and pass it a string we would like the sample to be labelled with.

Listing 5-21. Collecting samples

```
const redButton = document.getElementById("red");
redButton.onclick = async () => await transferRecognizer.
collectExample("red");
```

To start the training, we call the train method on the recognizer.

Listing 5-22. Training

```
const trainButton = document.getElementById("train");
trainButton.onclick = async () => {
  await transferRecognizer.train({
    epochs: 25,
```

```
    callback: {
      onEpochEnd: async (epoch, logs) => {
        console.log(`Epoch ${epoch}: loss=${logs.loss},
        accuracy=${logs.acc}`);
      },
    },
  });
};
```

And finally, to classify live audio inputs after training, we call the listen method.

Listing 5-23. Predict

```
const predictButton = document.getElementById("predict");
predictButton.onclick = async () => {
  await transferRecognizer.listen(
    (result) => {
      const words = transferRecognizer.wordLabels();
      for (let i = 0; i < words.length; ++i) {
        console.log(`score for word '${words[i]}' = ${result.
        scores[i]}`);
      }
    },
    { probabilityThreshold: 0.75 }
  );
};
```

Altogether, this code sample looks like the following.

Listing 5-24. Full code sample

```
let transferRecognizer;

const init = async () => {
  const baseRecognizer = speechCommands.create("BROWSER_FFT");
  await baseRecognizer.ensureModelLoaded();
  transferRecognizer = baseRecognizer.createTransfer("colors");
};

init();


const redButton = document.getElementById("red");
const backgroundButton = document.getElementById("background");
const trainButton = document.getElementById("train");
const predictButton = document.getElementById("predict");

redButton.onclick = async () => await transferRecognizer.
collectExample("red");

backgroundButton.onclick = async () =>
  await transferRecognizer.collectExample("_background_
  noise_");

trainButton.onclick = async () => {
  await transferRecognizer.train({
    epochs: 25,
    callback: {
      onEpochEnd: async (epoch, logs) => {
        console.log(`Epoch ${epoch}: loss=${logs.loss},
        accuracy=${logs.acc}`);
      },
```

```
    },
  });
};

predictButton.onclick = async () => {
  await transferRecognizer.listen(
    (result) => {
      const words = transferRecognizer.wordLabels();
      for (let i = 0; i < words.length; ++i) {
        console.log(`score for word '${words[i]}' = ${result.
        scores[i]}`);
      }
    },
    { probabilityThreshold: 0.75 }
  );
};
```

5.1.7 Applications

Even though the examples I have used so far for our code samples (speaking and coughing) might have seemed simple, the way this technology is currently being used shows how interesting it can be.

Health

In July 2020, Apple announced the release of a new version of their watchOS that included an application triggering a countdown when the user washes their hands. Related to the advice from public health officials around avoiding the spread of COVID-19, this application uses the watch's microphone to detect the sound of running water and trigger the 20 seconds countdown.

Figure 5-18. *Countdown triggered when the user washes their hands*

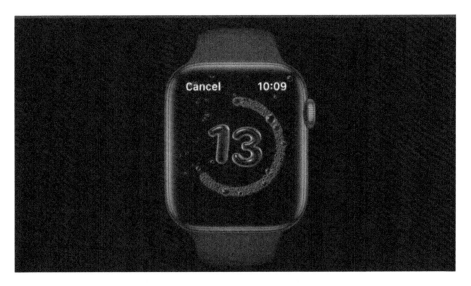

Figure 5-19. *Interface of the countdown on the Apple Watch*

From the code samples shown in the last few pages, a similar application can be built using JavaScript and TensorFlow.js.

Figure 5-20. *Prototype of similar countdown interface using TensorFlow.js*

Biodiversity research and protection

One of my favorite applications for this technology is in biodiversity research and protection of endangered species.

A really good example of this is the Rainforest Connection collective.

This collective uses old cell phone and their built-in microphones to detect the sound of chainsaws in the forest and alert rangers of potential activities of illegal deforestation.

Using solar panels and attaching the installation to trees, they can constantly monitor what is going on around and run live predictions.

Figure 5-21. *Example of installation made of solar panels and used mobile phones. Source: https://www.facebook.com/RainforestCx/*

If this is a project that interests you, they also have a mobile application called Rainforest Connection, in which you can listen to the sound of nature, live from the forest, if you would like to check it out!

Another use of this technology is in protecting killer whales. A collaboration between Google, Rainforest Connection, and Fisheries and Oceans Canada (DFO) uses bioacoustics monitoring to track, monitor, and observe the animal's behavior in the Salish Sea.

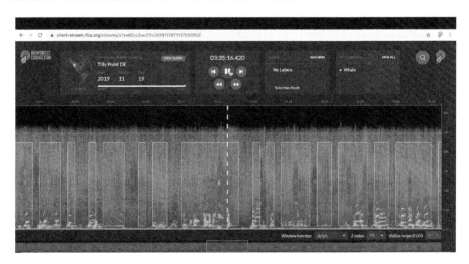

Figure 5-22. *Web interface tracking killer whales. Source: https://venturebeat.com/2020/01/28/googles-ai-powers-real-time-orca-tracking-in-vancouver-bay/*

Web Accessibility

Another application you might not have noticed is currently implemented in a service you probably know. Indeed, if you are using YouTube, you may have come across **live ambient sound captioning**.

If you have ever activated captions on a YouTube video, you may know of spoken words being displayed as an overlay at the bottom.

However, there are more information in a video than what can be found in the transcripts.

Indeed, people without hearing impairment benefit from having access to additional information in the form of contextual sounds like music playing or the sound of rain in a video.

Only displaying spoken words in captions can cut quite a lot of information out for people with hearing impairment.

About 3 years ago, in 2017, YouTube released live ambient sound captioning that uses acoustic recognition to add to the captions details about ambient sounds detected in the soundtrack of a video.

Here is an example.

Figure 5-23. *Example of live ambient sound captioning on YouTube*

The preceding screenshot is taken from an interview between Janelle Monae and Pharrell Williams where the captions are activated.

Spoken words are displayed as expected, but we can also see ambient sounds like [Applause].

People with hearing impairment can now have the opportunity to get more information about the video than only dialogues.

At the moment, the ambient sounds that can be detected on YouTube videos include

- Applause

- Music playing

- Laughter

It might not seem like much, but again, this is something we take for granted if we never have to think about the experience some people with disabilities have on these platforms.

Besides, thinking this feature has been implemented about 3 years ago already shows that a major technology company like Google has been actively exploring the potential of using machine learning with audio data and has been working on finding useful applications.

5.1.8 Limits

Now that we covered how to experiment with acoustic activity recognition in JavaScript and a few different applications, it is important to be aware of some of the limitations of such technology to have a better understanding of the real opportunities.

Quality and quantity of the data

If you decide to build a similar acoustic activity recognition system from scratch and write your own model without using transfer learning and the speech commands model from TensorFlow.js, you are going to need to collect a lot more sound samples than the minimum of 8 required when using Teachable Machine.

To gather a large amount of samples, you can either decide to record them yourself or buy them from a professional audio library.

Another important point is to make sure to check the quality of the data recorded. If you want to detect the sound of a vacuum cleaner running, for example, make sure that there is no background noise and that the vacuum cleaner can be clearly heard in the audio track.

One tip to generate samples of data from a single one is to use an audio editing software to change some parameters of a single audio source to create multiple versions of it. You can, for example, modify the reverb, the pitch, and so on.

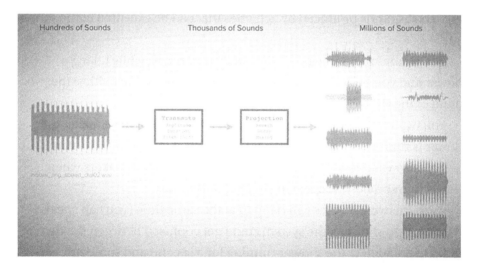

Figure 5-24. *Transforming sounds. Gierad Laput, Karan Ahuja, Mayank Goel, and Chris Harrison. 2018. Ubicoustics: Plug-and-Play Acoustic Activity Recognition. In The 31st Annual ACM Symposium on User Interface Software and Technology (UIST '18). ACM, New York, NY, USA, 213-224. DOI:* `https://doi.org/10.1145/3242587.3242609`

Single activity

At the moment, this technology seems to be efficient in recognizing a single sound at once.

For example, if you trained your model to recognize the sound of someone speaking as well as the sound of running water, if you placed your system in the kitchen and the user was speaking as well as washing the dishes, the activity predicted would only be the one with the highest score in the predictions returned.

However, as the system runs continuously, it would probably get confused between the two activities. It would probably alternate between "speaking" and "running water" until one of the activities stopped.

This would definitely become a problem if you built an application that can detect sounds produced by activities that can be executed at the same time.

For example, let's imagine you usually play music while taking a shower and you built an application that can detect two activities: the sound of the shower running and speaking.

You want to be able to trigger a counter whenever it detects that the shower is running so you can avoid taking long showers and save water.

You also want to be able to lower the sound of your speakers when it detects that someone is speaking in the bathroom.

As these two activities can happen at the same time (you can speak while taking a shower), the system could get confused between the two activities and detect the shower running for a second and someone speaking the next.

As a result, it would start and stop the speakers one second, and start/stop the counter the next. This would definitely not create an ideal experience.

However, this does not mean that there is no potential in building applications using acoustic activity recognition, it only means that we would need to work around this limitation.

Besides, some research is being done around developing systems that can handle the detection of multiple activities at once. We will look into it in the next few pages.

User experience

When it comes to user experience, there are always some challenges with new technologies like this one.

First of all, **privacy**.

Having devices listening to users always raises some concerns about where the data is stored, how it is used, is it secure, and so on.

Considering that some companies releasing Internet of Things devices do not always put security first in their products, these concerns are very normal.

As a result, the adoption of these devices by consumers can be slower than expected.

Not only privacy and security should be baked in these systems, it should also be communicated to users in a clear way to reassure them and give them a sense of empowerment over their data.

Secondly, another challenge is in teaching users **new interactions**.

For example, even though most modern phones now have voice assistants built-in, getting information from asking Siri or Google is not the primary interaction.

This could be for various reasons including privacy and limitations of the technology itself, but people also have habits that are difficult to change.

Besides, considering the current imperfect state of this technology, it is easy for users to give up after a few trials, when they do not get the response they were looking for.

A way to mitigate this would be to release small applications to analyze users' reactions to them and adapt. The work Apple did by implementing the water detection in their new watchOS is an example of that.

Finally, one of the big challenges of creating a custom acoustic activity recognition system is in the **collection of sample data and training by the users**.

Even though you can build and release an application that detects the sound of a faucet running because there's a high probability that it produces a similar sound in most homes, some other sounds are not so common.

As a result, empowering users to use this technology would involve letting them record their own samples and train the model so they can have the opportunity to have a customized application.

However, as machine learning algorithms need to be trained with a large amount of data to have a chance to produce accurate predictions, it would require a lot of effort from users and would inevitably not be successful.

Luckily, some researchers are experimenting with solutions to these problems.

Now, even though there are some limits to this technology, solutions also start to appear.

For example, in terms of protecting users' privacy, an open source project called Project Alias by Bjørn Karmann attempts to empower voice assistant users.

This project is a DIY add-on made with a Raspberry Pi microcontroller, a speaker, and microphone module, all in a 3D printed enclosure that aims at blocking voice assistants like Amazon Alexa and Google Home from continuously listening to people.

Through a mobile application, users can train Alias to react on a custom wake word or sound. Once it is trained, Alias can take control over the home assistant and activate it for you. When you don't use it, the add-on will prevent the assistant from listening by emitting white noise into their microphone.

Alias's neural network being run locally, the privacy of the user is protected.

Figure 5-25. *Project Alias. Source:* `https://bjoernkarmann.dk/ project_alias`

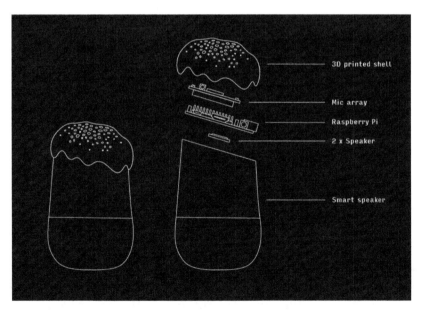

Figure 5-26. *Project Alias components. Source:* `https:// bjoernkarmann.dk/project_alias`

Another project, called Synthetic Sensors, aims at creating a system that can accurately predict multiple sounds at once.

Developed by a team of researchers at the Carnegie Mellon University, this project involves a custom-built piece of hardware made of multiple sensors, including an accelerometer, microphone, temperature sensor, motion sensor, and color sensor.

Using the raw data collected from these sensors, researchers created multiple stacked spectrograms and trained algorithms to detect patterns produced by multiple activities such as

- Microwave door closed

- Wood saw running

- Kettle on

- Faucet running

- Toilet flushing

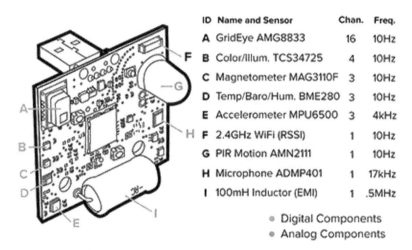

ID	Name and Sensor	Chan.	Freq.
A	GridEye AMG8833	16	10Hz
B	Color/Illum. TCS34725	4	10Hz
C	Magnetometer MAG3110F	3	10Hz
D	Temp/Baro/Hum. BME280	3	10Hz
E	Accelerometer MPU6500	3	4kHz
F	2.4GHz WiFi (RSSI)	1	10Hz
G	PIR Motion AMN2111	1	10Hz
H	Microphone ADMP401	1	17kHz
I	100mH Inductor (EMI)	1	.5MHz

- Digital Components
- Analog Components

Figure 5-27. *Project Synthetic Sensors hardware. Gierad Laput, Yang Zhang, and Chris Harrison. 2017. Synthetic Sensors: Towards General-Purpose Sensing. In Proceedings of the 2017 CHI Conference on Human Factors in Computing Systems (CHI '17). ACM, New York, NY, USA, 3986-3999. DOI:* `https://doi.org/10.1145/3025453.3025773`*.*

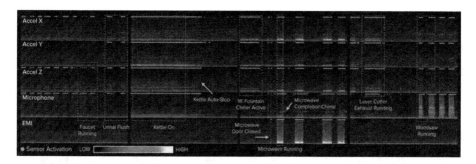

Figure 5-28. *Project Synthetic Sensors example of spectrograms and activities recognition. Gierad Laput, Yang Zhang, and Chris Harrison. 2017. Synthetic Sensors: Towards General-Purpose Sensing. In Proceedings of the 2017 CHI Conference on Human Factors in Computing Systems (CHI '17). ACM, New York, NY, USA, 3986-3999. DOI: https://doi.org/10.1145/3025453.3025773*

Finally, in terms of user experience, a research project called Listen Learner aims at allowing users to collect data and train a model to recognize custom sounds, with minimal effort.

The full name of the project is Listen Learner, Automatic Class Discovery and One-Shot Interaction for Activity Recognition.

It aims at providing high classification accuracy, while minimizing user burden, by continuously listening to sounds in its environment, classifying them by cluster of similar sounds, and asking the user what the sound is after having collected enough similar samples.

The result of the study shows that this system can accurately and automatically learn acoustic events (e.g., 97% precision, 87% recall), while adhering to users' preferences for nonintrusive interactive behavior.

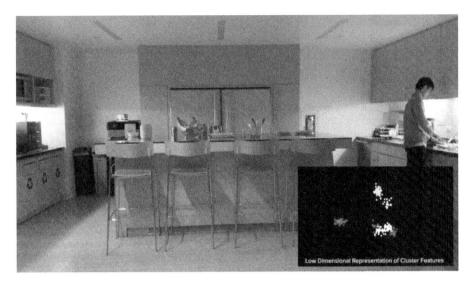

Figure 5-29. *Wu, J., Harrison, C., Bigham, J. and Laput, G. 2020. Automated Class Discovery and One-Shot Interactions for Acoustic Activity Recognition. In Proceedings of the 38th Annual SIGCHI Conference on Human Factors in Computing Systems. CHI '20. ACM, New York, NY. Source:* www.chrisharrison.net/index.php/ Research/ListenLearner

5.2 Body and movement tracking

After looking at how to use machine learning with audio data, let's look into another type of input, that is, body tracking.

In this section, we are going to use data from body movements via the webcam using three different Tensorlfow.js models.

5.2.1 Facemesh

The first model we are going to experiment with is called Facemesh. It is a machine learning model focused on face recognition that predicts the position of 486 3D facial landmarks on a user's face, returning points with their x, y, and z coordinates.

Figure 5-30. *Example of visualization of face tracking with Facemesh. source:* `https://github.com/tensorflow/tfjs-models/tree/master/facemesh`

Figure 5-31. *Map of the keypoints. Source:* `https://github.com/`
`tensorflow/tfjs-models/tree/master/facemesh`

The main difference between this face recognition model and other face tracking JavaScript libraries like face-tracking.js is that the TensorFlow.js model intends to approximate the surface geometry of a human face and not only the 2D position of some key points.

This model provides coordinates in a 3D environment which allows to approximate the depth of facial features as well as tracking the position of key points even when the user is rotating their face in three dimensions.

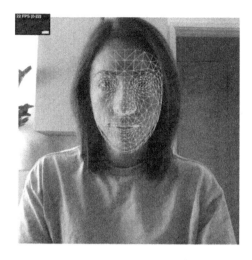
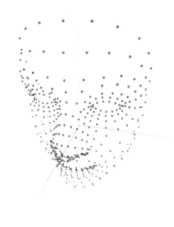

Figure 5-32. *Key points using the webcam and in a 3D visualization. Source: https://storage.googleapis.com/tfjs-models/demos/ facemesh/index.html*

Loading the model

To start using the model, we need to load it using the two following lines in your HTML file.

Listing 5-25. Importing TensorFlow.js and Facemesh in an HTML file

```
<script src="https://cdn.jsdelivr.net/npm/@tensorflow/tfjs">
</script>
<script src='https://cdn.jsdelivr.net/npm/@tensorflow-models/
facemesh'></script>
```

As we are going to use the video feed from the webcam to detect faces, we also need to add a video element to our file.

Altogether, the very minimum HTML you need for this is as follows.

Listing 5-26. Core HTML code needed

```
<html lang="en">
  <head>
    <meta charset="UTF-8" />
    <meta name="viewport" content="width=device-width,
    initial-scale=1.0" />
    <title>Facemesh</title>
  </head>
  <body>

    <video></video>

    <script src="https://cdn.jsdelivr.net/npm/@tensorflow/
    tfjs"></script>
    <script src="https://cdn.jsdelivr.net/npm/@tensorflow-
    models/facemesh"></script>
    <script src="index.js"></script>
  </body>
</html>
```

Then, in your JavaScript code, you need to load the model and the webcam feed using the following code.

Listing 5-27. Load the model and set up the webcam feed

```
let model;
let video;
const init = async () => {
  model = await facemesh.load();
  video = await loadVideo();
  main(); // This will be declared in the next code sample.
}
```

```
const loadVideo = async () => {
  const video = await setupCamera();
  video.play();
  return video;
};

const setupCamera = async () => {
  if (!navigator.mediaDevices || !navigator.mediaDevices.
  getUserMedia) {
    throw new Error(
      "Browser API navigator.mediaDevices.getUserMedia not
      available"
    );
  }

  video = document.querySelector("video");

  video.width = window.innerWidth;
  video.height = window.innerHeight;

  const stream = await navigator.mediaDevices.getUserMedia({
    audio: false,
    video: {
      facingMode: "user",
      width: window.innerWidth,
      height: window.innerHeight,
    },
  });
  video.srcObject = stream;

  return new Promise(
    (resolve) => (video.onloadedmetadata = () =>
    resolve(video))
  );
};
```

Predictions

Once the model and the video are ready, we can call our main function to find facial landmarks in the input stream.

Listing 5-28. Function to find face landmarks

```
async function main() {
  const predictions = await model.estimateFaces(
    document.querySelector("video")
  );

  if (predictions.length > 0) {
    console.log(predictions);

    for (let i = 0; i < predictions.length; i++) {
      const keypoints = predictions[i].scaledMesh;

      // Log facial keypoints.
      for (let i = 0; i < keypoints.length; i++) {
        const [x, y, z] = keypoints[i];

        console.log(`Keypoint ${i}: [${x}, ${y}, ${z}]`);
      }
    }
  }
}
```

The output of this code sample in the browser's console returns the following.

index.js:59

▼ [{…}] ⓘ
  ▼ 0:
    ▼ annotations:
      ▶ leftCheek: [Array(3)]
      ▶ leftEyeLower0: (9) [Array(3), Array(3), Array(3), Array(3), Array(3), Array(3), Arra…
      ▶ leftEyeLower1: (9) [Array(3), Array(3), Array(3), Array(3), Array(3), Array(3), Arra…
      ▶ leftEyeLower2: (9) [Array(3), Array(3), Array(3), Array(3), Array(3), Array(3), Arra…
      ▶ leftEyeLower3: (9) [Array(3), Array(3), Array(3), Array(3), Array(3), Array(3), Arra…
      ▶ leftEyeUpper0: (7) [Array(3), Array(3), Array(3), Array(3), Array(3), Array(3), Arra…
      ▶ leftEyeUpper1: (7) [Array(3), Array(3), Array(3), Array(3), Array(3), Array(3), Arra…
      ▶ leftEyeUpper2: (7) [Array(3), Array(3), Array(3), Array(3), Array(3), Array(3), Arra…
      ▶ leftEyebrowLower: (6) [Array(3), Array(3), Array(3), Array(3), Array(3), Array(3)]
      ▶ leftEyebrowUpper: (8) [Array(3), Array(3), Array(3), Array(3), Array(3), Array(3), A…
      ▶ lipsLowerInner: (11) [Array(3), Array(3), Array(3), Array(3), Array(3), Array(3), Ar…
      ▶ lipsLowerOuter: (10) [Array(3), Array(3), Array(3), Array(3), Array(3), Array(3), Ar…
      ▶ lipsUpperInner: (11) [Array(3), Array(3), Array(3), Array(3), Array(3), Array(3), Ar…
      ▶ lipsUpperOuter: (11) [Array(3), Array(3), Array(3), Array(3), Array(3), Array(3), Ar…
      ▶ midwayBetweenEyes: [Array(3)]
      ▶ noseBottom: [Array(3)]
      ▶ noseLeftCorner: [Array(3)]
      ▶ noseRightCorner: [Array(3)]
      ▶ noseTip: [Array(3)]
      ▶ rightCheek: [Array(3)]
      ▶ rightEyeLower0: (9) [Array(3), Array(3), Array(3), Array(3), Array(3), Array(3), Arr…
      ▶ rightEyeLower1: (9) [Array(3), Array(3), Array(3), Array(3), Array(3), Array(3), Arr…
      ▶ rightEyeLower2: (9) [Array(3), Array(3), Array(3), Array(3), Array(3), Array(3), Arr…
      ▶ rightEyeLower3: (9) [Array(3), Array(3), Array(3), Array(3), Array(3), Array(3), Arr…
      ▶ rightEyeUpper0: (7) [Array(3), Array(3), Array(3), Array(3), Array(3), Array(3), Arr…
      ▶ rightEyeUpper1: (7) [Array(3), Array(3), Array(3), Array(3), Array(3), Array(3), Arr…
      ▶ rightEyeUpper2: (7) [Array(3), Array(3), Array(3), Array(3), Array(3), Array(3), Arr…
      ▶ rightEyebrowLower: (6) [Array(3), Array(3), Array(3), Array(3), Array(3), Array(3)]
      ▶ rightEyebrowUpper: (8) [Array(3), Array(3), Array(3), Array(3), Array(3), Array(3), …
      ▶ silhouette: (36) [Array(3), Array(3), Array(3), Array(3), Array(3), Array(3), Array(…
      ▶ __proto__: Object
    ▼ boundingBox:
      ▶ bottomRight: [Array(2)]
      ▶ topLeft: [Array(2)]
      ▶ __proto__: Object
      faceInViewConfidence: 1
    ▶ mesh: (468) [Array(3), Array(3), Array(3), Array(3), Array(3), Array(3), Array(3), Ar…
    ▶ scaledMesh: (468) [Array(3), Array(3), Array(3), Array(3), Array(3), Array(3), Array(…
    ▶ __proto__: Object
    length: 1
  ▶ __proto__: Array(0)

Figure 5-33. *Output of the landmarks in the console*

```
Keypoint 0: [318.84686279296875, 333.2689208984375, -17.73261260986328]
Keypoint 1: [318.8270263671875, 286.3834228515625, -31.85231590270996]
Keypoint 2: [317.3210144042969, 300.437744140625, -16.70516014099121]
Keypoint 3: [305.3751220703125, 243.38858032226562, -24.32175636291504]
Keypoint 4: [318.4298400878906, 272.6722106933594, -33.91924285888672]
Keypoint 5: [316.829833984375, 255.093505859375, -31.484174728393555]
Keypoint 6: [312.1591796875, 212.55194091796875, -15.220454216003418]
Keypoint 7: [225.24191284179688, 213.94921875, 4.484597682952881]
Keypoint 8: [309.7986755371094, 177.85330200195312, -11.275860786437988]
Keypoint 9: [309.076171875, 158.97671508789062, -12.5580472946167]
Keypoint 10: [305.1268310546875, 94.13230895996094, -5.912814140319824]
Keypoint 11: [319.073974609375, 340.114990234375, -16.97875213623047]
Keypoint 12: [318.939208984375, 345.65545654296875, -14.827878952026367]
Keypoint 13: [318.5044860839844, 348.13134765625, -12.05972957611084]
Keypoint 14: [318.70220947265625, 354.124755859375, -11.066083908081055]
Keypoint 15: [319.1364440917969, 360.4091796875, -11.916581153869629]
Keypoint 16: [319.45709228515625, 368.2342529296875, -12.95324420928955]
Keypoint 17: [319.48004150390625, 376.0826416015625, -11.676970481872559]
Keypoint 18: [318.7998046875, 386.280517578125, -5.23903751373291]
Keypoint 19: [318.501708984375, 293.18817138671875, -28.807281494140625]
Keypoint 20: [307.4814147949219, 293.11370849609375, -20.99542999267578]
Keypoint 21: [179.48655700683594, 163.22711181640625, 31.125228881835938]
Keypoint 22: [259.3016357421875, 224.5801544189453, -0.5516967177391052]
Keypoint 23: [247.83482360839844, 226.4242706298828, -0.5922013521194458]
Keypoint 24: [236.79103088378906, 226.1751251220703, 0.6633090972900391]
Keypoint 25: [221.40748596191406, 219.16049194335938, 5.207747459411621]
Keypoint 26: [269.01507568359375, 220.50030517578125, 0.6695229411125183]
Keypoint 27: [242.87081909179688, 189.46180725097656, -3.4604973793029785]
Keypoint 28: [255.5243377685547, 189.9107666015625, -2.8217029571533203]
Keypoint 29: [231.16587829589844, 192.13162231445312, -1.8839000463485718]
Keypoint 30: [223.3328857421875, 197.36083984375, 0.35333529114723206]
Keypoint 31: [212.8154754638672, 228.43931579589844, 7.960582733154297]
Keypoint 32: [276.8365478515625, 405.1337890625, -0.10506264865398407]
Keypoint 33: [221.00311279296875, 210.57061767578125, 6.307644367218018]
Keypoint 34: [178.00701904296875, 221.76185607910156, 33.09210205078125]
Keypoint 35: [199.2740478515625, 218.75218200683594, 13.564780235290527]
Keypoint 36: [256.8660888671875, 280.37115478515625, -6.076208591461182]
Keypoint 37: [305.32379150390625, 332.184814453125, -17.462400436401367]
Keypoint 38: [307.801025390625, 346.38592529296875, -14.566855430603027]
Keypoint 39: [291.48431396484375, 338.322021484375, -14.701850891113281]
Keypoint 40: [282.71435546875, 345.22100830078125, -11.098549842834473]
```

Figure 5-34. *Output of loop statement in the console*

190

As we can see in the preceding two screenshots, the predictions returned contain an important amount of information.

The annotations are organized by landmark areas, in alphabetical order and containing arrays of x, y, and z coordinates.

The bounding box contains two main keys, `bottomRight` and `topLeft`, to indicate the boundaries of the position of the detected face in the video stream. These two properties contain an array of only two coordinates, x and y, as the z axis is not useful in this case.

Finally, the `mesh` and `scaledMesh` properties contain all coordinates of the landmarks and are useful to render all points in 3D space on the screen.

Full code sample

Altogether, the JavaScript code to set up the model, the video feed, and start predicting the position of landmarks should look like the following.

Listing 5-29. Full JavaScript code sample

```
let video;
let model;

const init = async () => {
  video = await loadVideo();
  await tf.setBackend("webgl");
  model = await facemesh.load();
  main();
};

const loadVideo = async () => {
  const video = await setupCamera();
  video.play();
  return video;
};
```

```
const setupCamera = async () => {
  if (!navigator.mediaDevices || !navigator.mediaDevices.
  getUserMedia) {
    throw new Error(
      "Browser API navigator.mediaDevices.getUserMedia not
      available"
    );
  }

  video = document.querySelector("video");

  video.width = window.innerWidth;
  video.height = window.innerHeight;

  const stream = await navigator.mediaDevices.getUserMedia({
    audio: false,
    video: {
      facingMode: "user",
      width: window.innerWidth,
      height: window.innerHeight,
    },
  });
  video.srcObject = stream;

  return new Promise(
    (resolve) => (video.onloadedmetadata = () =>
resolve(video))
  );
};
```

```
init();

async function main() {
  const predictions = await model.estimateFaces(
    document.querySelector("video")
  );

  if (predictions.length > 0) {
    console.log(predictions);

    for (let i = 0; i < predictions.length; i++) {
      const keypoints = predictions[i].scaledMesh;

      // Log facial keypoints.
      for (let i = 0; i < keypoints.length; i++) {
        const [x, y, z] = keypoints[i];

        console.log(`Keypoint ${i}: [${x}, ${y}, ${z}]`);
      }
    }
  }
  requestAnimationFrame(main);
}
```

Project

To put this code sample into practice, let's build a quick prototype to allow users to scroll down a page by tilting their head back and forth.

We are going to be able to reuse most of the code written previously and make some small modifications to trigger a scroll using some of the landmarks detected.

The specific landmark we are going to use to detect the movement of the head is the lipsLowerOuter and more precisely its z axis.

Looking at all the properties available in the annotations object, using the lipsLowerOuter one is the closest to the chin, so we can look at the predicted changes of z coordinate for this area to determine if the head is tilting backward (chin moving forward) or forward (chin moving backward).

To do this, in our main function, once we get predictions, we can add the following lines of code.

Listing 5-30. Triggering scroll when z axis changes

```
if (predictions[0].annotations.lipsLowerOuter) {
   let zAxis = predictions[0].annotations.lipsLowerOuter[9][2];

   if (zAxis > 5) {
     // Scroll down
     window.scrollTo({
       top: (scrollPosition += 10),
       left: 0,
       behavior: "smooth",
     });
   } else if (zAxis < -5) {
     // Scroll up
     window.scrollTo({
      top: (scrollPosition -= 10),
      left: 0,
      behavior: "smooth",
    });
   }
}
```

In this code sample, I declare a variable that I call zAxis to store the value of the z coordinate I want to track. To get this value, I look into the array of coordinates contained in the lipsLowerOuter property of the annotations object.

Based on the annotation objects returned, we can see that the
`lipsLowerOuter` property contains 10 arrays of 3 values each.

index.js:59
▼ {silhouette: Array(36), lipsUpperOuter: Array(11), lipsLowerOuter: Array
  (10), lipsUpperInner: Array(11), lipsLowerInner: Array(11), …} 🔳
  ▶ leftCheek: [Array(3)]
  ▶ leftEyeLower0: (9) [Array(3), Array(3), Array(3), Array(3), Array(3), …
  ▶ leftEyeLower1: (9) [Array(3), Array(3), Array(3), Array(3), Array(3), …
  ▶ leftEyeLower2: (9) [Array(3), Array(3), Array(3), Array(3), Array(3), …
  ▶ leftEyeLower3: (9) [Array(3), Array(3), Array(3), Array(3), Array(3), …
  ▶ leftEyeUpper0: (7) [Array(3), Array(3), Array(3), Array(3), Array(3), …
  ▶ leftEyeUpper1: (7) [Array(3), Array(3), Array(3), Array(3), Array(3), …
  ▶ leftEyeUpper2: (7) [Array(3), Array(3), Array(3), Array(3), Array(3), …
  ▶ leftEyebrowLower: (6) [Array(3), Array(3), Array(3), Array(3), Array(3…
  ▶ leftEyebrowUpper: (8) [Array(3), Array(3), Array(3), Array(3), Array(3…
  ▶ lipsLowerInner: (11) [Array(3), Array(3), Array(3), Array(3), Array(3)…
  ▼ lipsLowerOuter: Array(10)
    ▶ 0: (3) [368.00274658203125, 392.34881591796875, -9.324745178222656]
    ▶ 1: (3) [374.396728515625, 396.18389892578125, -13.169844627380371]
    ▶ 2: (3) [384.5598449707031, 401.2203369140625, -15.978527069091797]
    ▶ 3: (3) [397.68927001953125, 404.5028076171875, -18.30223846435547]
    ▶ 4: (3) [412.7346496582031, 404.46710205078125, -18.818143844604492]
    ▶ 5: (3) [427.6860656738281, 402.327880859375, -18.53829574584961]
    ▶ 6: (3) [440.1507568359375, 397.0994873046875, -16.3538761138916]
    ▶ 7: (3) [449.3558349609375, 390.53314208984375, -13.628349304199219]
    ▶ 8: (3) [455.0732116699219, 385.7010498046875, -9.793708801269531]
    ▶ 9: (3) [458.38330078125, 381.10955810546875, -6.075018405914307]
      length: 10
    ▶ __proto__: Array(0)
  ▶ lipsUpperInner: (11) [Array(3), Array(3), Array(3), Array(3), Array(3)…
  ▶ lipsUpperOuter: (11) [Array(3), Array(3), Array(3), Array(3), Array(3)…
  ▶ midwayBetweenEyes: [Array(3)]

Figure 5-35. *Annotations returned with lipsLowerOuter values*

This is why the code sample shown just earlier was accessing the z
coordinates using `predictions[0].annotations.lipsLowerOuter[9][2]`.

I decided to access the last element ([9]) of the `lipsLowerOuter`
property and its third value ([2]), the z coordinate of the section.

The value 5 was selected after trial and error and seeing what threshold
would work for this particular project. It is not a standard value that you
will need to use every time you use the Facemesh model. Instead,

I decided it was the correct threshold for me to use after logging the variable `zAxis` and seeing its value change in the browser's console as I was tilting my head back and forth.

Then, assuming that you declared `scrollPosition` earlier in the code and set it to a value (I personally set it to 0), a "scroll up" event will happen when you tilt your head backward and "scroll down" when you tilt your head forward.

Finally, I set the property `behavior` to "smooth" so we have some smooth scrolling happening, which, in my opinion, creates a better experience.

If you did not add any content to your HTML file, you won't see anything happen yet though, so don't forget to add enough text or images to be able to test that everything is working!

In less than 75 lines of JavaScript, we loaded a face recognition model, set up the video stream, ran predictions to get the 3D coordinates of facial landmarks, and wrote some logic to trigger a scroll up or down when tilting your head backward or forward!

Listing 5-31. Complete JavaScript code

```
let video;
let model;

const init = async () => {
  video = await loadVideo();
  await tf.setBackend("webgl");
  model = await facemesh.load();
  main();
};

const loadVideo = async () => {
  const video = await setupCamera();
  video.play();
```

```
    return video;
};

const setupCamera = async () => {
  if (!navigator.mediaDevices || !navigator.mediaDevices.
  getUserMedia) {
    throw new Error(
      "Browser API navigator.mediaDevices.getUserMedia not
      available"
    );
  }

  video = document.querySelector("video");
  video.width = window.innerWidth;
  video.height = window.innerHeight;

  const stream = await navigator.mediaDevices.getUserMedia({
    audio: false,
    video: {
      facingMode: "user",
      width: window.innerWidth,
      height: window.innerHeight,
    },
  });
  video.srcObject = stream;

  return new Promise(
    (resolve) => (video.onloadedmetadata = () =>
resolve(video))
  );
};
```

```
init();

let scrollPosition = 0;

async function main() {
  const predictions = await model.estimateFaces(
    document.querySelector("video")
  );

  if (predictions.length > 0) {
    if (predictions[0].annotations.lipsLowerOuter) {
      zAxis = predictions[0].annotations.lipsLowerOuter[9][2];

      if (zAxis > 5) {
        // Scroll down
        window.scrollTo({
          top: (scrollPosition += 10),
          left: 0,
          behavior: "smooth",
        });
      } else if (zAxis < -5) {
        // Scroll up
        window.scrollTo({
          top: (scrollPosition -= 10),
          left: 0,
          behavior: "smooth",
        });
      }
    }
  }
  requestAnimationFrame(main);
}
```

This model is specialized in detecting face landmarks. Next, we're going to look into another one, to detect keypoints in a user's hands.

5.2.2 Handpose

The second model we are going to experiment with is called Handpose. This model specializes in recognizing the position of 21 3D keypoints in the user's hands.

The following is an example of the output of this model, once visualized on the screen using the Canvas API.

Figure 5-36. *Keypoints from Handpose visualized. Source:* `https://github.com/tensorflow/tfjs-models/tree/master/handpose`

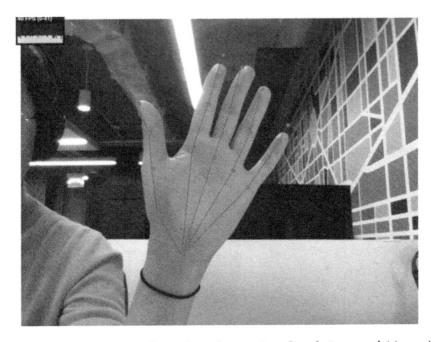

Figure 5-37. Keypoints from Handpose visualized. Source: https://github.com/tensorflow/tfjs-models/tree/master/handpose

To implement this, the lines of code will look very familiar if you have read the previous section.

Loading the model

We need to start by requiring TensorFlow.js and the Handpose model:

Listing 5-32. Import TensorFlow.js and the Handpose model

```
<script src="https://cdn.jsdelivr.net/npm/@tensorflow/tfjs">
</script>
<script src="https://cdn.jsdelivr.net/npm/@tensorflow-models/
handpose"></script>
```

Similarly to the way the Facemesh model works, we are going to use the video stream as input so we also need to add a video element in your main HTML file.

Then, in your JavaScript file, we can use the same functions we wrote before to set up the camera and load the model. The only line we will need to change is the line where we call the load method on the model.

As we are using Handpose instead of Facemesh, we need to replace `facemesh.load()` with `handpose.load()`.

So, overall the base of your JavaScript file should have the following code.

Listing 5-33. Code to set up to load the model and video input

```
let video;
let model;

const init = async () => {
  video = await loadVideo();
  await tf.setBackend("webgl");
  model = await handpose.load();
};

const loadVideo = async () => {
  const video = await setupCamera();
  video.play();
  return video;
};

const setupCamera = async () => {
  if (!navigator.mediaDevices || !navigator.mediaDevices.
  getUserMedia) {
    throw new Error(
      "Browser API navigator.mediaDevices.getUserMedia not
      available"
    );
  }
```

```
video = document.querySelector("video");

video.width = window.innerWidth;
video.height = window.innerHeight;

const stream = await navigator.mediaDevices.getUserMedia({
  audio: false,
  video: {
    facingMode: "user",
    width: window.innerWidth,
    height: window.innerHeight,
  },
});
video.srcObject = stream;

return new Promise(
  (resolve) => (video.onloadedmetadata = () =>
  resolve(video))
);
};

init();
```

Predicting key points

Once the model is loaded and the webcam feed is set up, we can run predictions and detect keypoints when a hand is placed in front of the webcam.

To do this, we can copy the main() function we created when using Facemesh, but replace the expression model.estimateFaces with model.estimateHands.

As a result, the main function should be as follows.

Listing 5-34. Run predictions and log the output

```
async function main() {
  const predictions = await model.estimateHands(
    document.querySelector("video")
  );

  if (predictions.length > 0) {
    console.log(predictions);
  }
  requestAnimationFrame(main);
}
```

The output of this code will log the following data in the browser's console.

```
                                                          index.js:54
▼ [{…}] 🔢
  ▼ 0:
    ▼ annotations:
      ▶ indexFinger: (4) [Array(3), Array(3), Array(3), Array(3)]
      ▶ middleFinger: (4) [Array(3), Array(3), Array(3), Array(3)]
      ▶ palmBase: [Array(3)]
      ▶ pinky: (4) [Array(3), Array(3), Array(3), Array(3)]
      ▶ ringFinger: (4) [Array(3), Array(3), Array(3), Array(3)]
      ▶ thumb: (4) [Array(3), Array(3), Array(3), Array(3)]
      ▶ __proto__: Object
    ▼ boundingBox:
      ▶ bottomRight: (2) [1068.1751179097103, 640.930607006075]
      ▶ topLeft: (2) [495.7532242126925, 68.50871330905704]
      ▶ __proto__: Object
      handInViewConfidence: 0.9999735355377197
    ▼ landmarks: Array(21)
      ▶ 0: (3) [836.5641542184931, 562.8730760473907, 0.000162921845912933…
      ▶ 1: (3) [778.9113943655965, 542.9900231017415, -5.674712181091309]
      ▶ 2: (3) [731.5130408710689, 492.92240847857767, -8.058176040649414]
      ▶ 3: (3) [715.8513881886247, 441.4746544929053, -10.840057373046875]
      ▶ 4: (3) [712.9626501035788, 414.33653300984304, -13.027971267700195]
      ▶ 5: (3) [744.5313615936487, 399.5443644760661, 0.8547027111053467]
      ▶ 6: (3) [711.4957282834183, 343.2729876443262, -0.04856002330780029]
      ▶ 7: (3) [690.3269800798431, 301.0036782974954, -1.6492177248001099]
      ▶ 8: (3) [670.8500700387785, 263.8833370186605, -3.4433629512786865]
      ▶ 9: (3) [785.2820379318708, 379.3556140481233, -0.8434169292449951]
      ▶ 10: (3) [759.0732681608662, 311.2425022796793, -0.5922948122024536]
      ▶ 11: (3) [738.5079951685206, 258.15817537493876, -2.977093458175659]
      ▶ 12: (3) [721.0362216256607, 215.9507162310162, -4.591973304748535]
      ▶ 13: (3) [828.4071783530605, 378.82989301831816, -4.102674007415771…
      ▶ 14: (3) [815.4685409389676, 312.2766152639716, -5.825711250305176]
      ▶ 15: (3) [802.14852546964, 261.10832828012525, -8.389548301696777]
      ▶ 16: (3) [789.860461166241, 218.3722992580373, -10.017251968383789]
      ▶ 17: (3) [874.8136664297696, 398.0993690479791, -8.415899276733398]
      ▶ 18: (3) [885.7451735928336, 344.85902281781944, -10.76519203186035…
      ▶ 19: (3) [891.0182862129919, 305.7525943940903, -12.65687084197998]
      ▶ 20: (3) [893.0782720836241, 266.1480072505441, -13.866006851196289]
        length: 21
```

Figure 5-38. *Output when detecting hands*

We can see that the format of this data is very similar to the one when using the Facemesh model!

This makes it easier and faster to experiment as you can reuse code samples you have written in other projects. It allows developers to get set up quickly to focus on experimenting with the possibilities of what can be built with such models, without spending too much time in configuration.

The main differences that can be noticed are the properties defined in annotations, the additional handInViewConfidence property, and the lack of mesh and scaledMesh data.

The handInViewConfidence property represents the probability of a hand being present. It is a floating value between 0 and 1. The closer it is to 1, the more confident the model is that a hand is found in the video stream.

At the moment of writing this book, this model is able to detect only one hand at a time. As a result, you cannot build applications that would require a user to use both hands at once as a way of interacting with the interface.

Full code sample

To check that everything is working properly, here is the full JavaScript code sample needed to test your setup.

Listing 5-35. Full code sample

```
let video;
let model;

const init = async () => {
  video = await loadVideo();
  await tf.setBackend("webgl");
  model = await handpose.load();
  main();
};
```

```
const loadVideo = async () => {
  const video = await setupCamera();
  video.play();
  return video;
};

const setupCamera = async () => {
  if (!navigator.mediaDevices || !navigator.mediaDevices.
  getUserMedia) {
    throw new Error(
      "Browser API navigator.mediaDevices.getUserMedia not
      available"
    );
  }

  video = document.querySelector("video");

  video.width = window.innerWidth;
  video.height = window.innerHeight;

  const stream = await navigator.mediaDevices.getUserMedia({
    audio: false,
    video: {
      facingMode: "user",
      width: window.innerWidth,
      height: window.innerHeight,
    },
  });
  video.srcObject = stream;
```

```
  return new Promise(
    (resolve) => (video.onloadedmetadata = () =>
    resolve(video))
  );
};

init();

async function main() {
  const predictions = await model.estimateHands(
    document.querySelector("video")
  );

  if (predictions.length > 0) {
    console.log(predictions);
  }
  requestAnimationFrame(main);
}
```

Project

To experiment with the kind of applications that can be built with this model, we're going to build a small "Rock Paper Scissors" game.

To understand how we are going to recognize the three gestures, let's have a look at the following visualizations to understand the position of the keypoints per gesture.

Figure 5-39. *"Rock" gesture visualized*

The preceding screenshot represents the "rock" gesture. As we can see, all fingers are folded so the tips of the fingers should be further in their z axis than the keypoint at the end of the first phalanx bone for each finger.

Otherwise, we can also consider that the y coordinate of the finger tips should be higher than the one of the major knuckles, keeping in mind that the top of the screen is equal to 0 and the lower the keypoint, the higher the y value.

We'll be able to play around with the data returned in the annotations object to see if this is accurate and can be used to detect the "rock" gesture.

Figure 5-40. *"Paper" gesture visualized*

In the "paper" gesture, all fingers are straight so we can use mainly the y coordinates of different fingers. For example, we could check if the y value of the last point of each finger (at the tips) is less than the y value of the palm or the base of each finger.

Figure 5-41. *"Scissors" gesture visualized*

Finally, the "scissors" gesture could be recognized by looking at the space in x axis between the index finger and the middle finger, as well as the y coordinate of the other fingers.

If the y value of the tip of the ring finger and little finger is lower than their base, they are probably folded.

Reusing the code samples we have gone through in the previous sections, let's look into how we can write the logic to recognize and differentiate these gestures.

If we start with the **"rock" gesture**, here is how we could check if the y coordinate of each finger is higher than the one of the base knuckle.

Listing 5-36. Logic to check if the index finger is folded

```
let indexBase = predictions[0].annotations.indexFinger[0][1];
let indexTip = predictions[0].annotations.indexFinger[3][1];

if (indexTip > indexBase) {
  console.log("index finger folded");
}
```

We can start by declaring two variables, one to store the y position of the base of the index finger and one for the tip of the same finger.

Looking back at the data from the annotations object when a finger is present on screen, we can see that, for the index finger, we get an array of 4 arrays representing the x, y, and z coordinates of each key point.

```
                                                           index.js:51
▼{thumb: Array(4), indexFinger: Array(4), middleFinger: Array(4), ringFing
 er: Array(4), pinky: Array(4), …} 🔲
  ▼indexFinger: Array(4)
    ▶0: (3) [637.2313842380053, 352.27317562181264, 3.435360908508301]
    ▶1: (3) [627.7352304765211, 256.52852524841035, -1.0732260942459106]
    ▶2: (3) [624.8677140995571, 186.5697348750417, -4.078496932983398]
    ▶3: (3) [625.0981624624536, 126.61715368783655, -6.065573692321777]
      length: 4
    ▶__proto__: Array(0)
  ▶middleFinger: (4) [Array(3), Array(3), Array(3), Array(3)]
  ▶palmBase: [Array(3)]
  ▶pinky: (4) [Array(3), Array(3), Array(3), Array(3)]
  ▶ringFinger: (4) [Array(3), Array(3), Array(3), Array(3)]
  ▶thumb: (4) [Array(3), Array(3), Array(3), Array(3)]
  ▶__proto__: Object
```

Figure 5-42. Output data when a hand is detected

The y coordinate in the first array has a value of about 352.27 and the y coordinate in the last array has a value of about 126.62, which is lower, so we can deduce that the first array represents the position of the base of the index finger, and the last array represents the keypoint at the tip of that finger.

We can test that this information is correct by writing the if statement shown earlier that logs the message "index finger folded" if the value of indexTip is higher than the one of indexBase.

And it works!

If you test this code by placing your hand in front of the camera and switch from holding your index finger straight and then folding it, you should see the message being logged in the console!

If we wanted to keep it really quick and simpler, we could stop here and decide that this single check determines the "rock" gesture. However, if we would like to have more confidence in our gesture, we could repeat the same process for the middle finger, ring finger, and little finger.

The thumb would be a little different as we would check the difference in x coordinate rather than y, because of the way this finger folds.

For the **"paper" gesture**, as all fingers are extended, we could check that the tip of each finger has a smaller y coordinate than the base.

Here's what the code could look like to verify that.

Listing 5-37. Check the y coordinate of each finger for the "paper" gesture

```
let indexBase = predictions[0].annotations.indexFinger[0][1];
let indexTip = predictions[0].annotations.indexFinger[3][1];

let thumbBase = predictions[0].annotations.thumb[0][1];
let thumbTip = predictions[0].annotations.thumb[3][1];

let middleBase = predictions[0].annotations.middleFinger[0][1];
let middleTip = predictions[0].annotations.middleFinger[3][1];

let ringBase = predictions[0].annotations.ringFinger[0][1];
let ringTip = predictions[0].annotations.ringFinger[3][1];

let pinkyBase = predictions[0].annotations.pinky[0][1];
let pinkyTip = predictions[0].annotations.pinky[3][1];
```

```
let indexExtended = indexBase > indexTip ? true : false;
let thumbExtended = thumbBase > thumbTip ? true : false;
let middleExtended = middleBase > middleTip ? true : false;
let ringExtended = ringBase > ringTip ? true : false;
let pinkyExtended = pinkyBase > pinkyTip ? true : false;

if (indexExtended && thumbExtended && middleExtended &&
ringExtended &&
    pinkyExtended) {
    console.log("paper gesture!");
  } else {
    console.log("other gesture");
  }
```

We start by storing the coordinates we are interested in into variables and then compare their values to set the extended states to true or false.

If all fingers are extended, we log the message "paper gesture!".

If everything is working fine, you should be able to place your hand in front of the camera with all fingers extended and see the logs in the browser's console.

If you change to another gesture, the message "other gesture" should be logged.

Figure 5-43. *Screenshot of hand detected in the webcam feed and paper gesture logged in the console*

Figure 5-44. *Screenshot of hand detected in the webcam feed and*
other gesture logged in the console

Finally, detecting the **"scissors" gesture** can be done by looking at the
changes of x coordinates for the tips of the index and middle fingers, as
well as making sure the other fingers are not extended.

Listing 5-38. Check the difference in x coordinate for the index and
middle finger tips

```
let indexTipX = predictions[0].annotations.indexFinger[3][0];
let middleTipX = predictions[0].annotations.middleFinger[3][0];

let diffFingersX =
    indexTipX > middleTipX ? indexTipX - middleTipX :
    middleTipX - indexTipX;
console.log(diffFingersX);
```

The following are two screenshots of the data we get back with this code sample.

```
11.034296375332246
11.539809567752513
11.072312060987997
10.39063982123264
11.586547650370449
9.024798036204402
7.630118302309825
6.248928732465629
8.00413890711593
7.874699597061294
12.088733585944851
9.731210751562116
8.369583255987095
20.17950780143576
22.64984324249201
38.513264911632405
49.588053248835536
97.95261135764486
130.3552236449617
126.82662143151674
136.73053218739722
141.2395397790143
141.8762550094267
148.37529246142583
153.42446674833252
155.9979232568311
157.1025430753176
159.6108134903027
155.54259919970195
157.64781056769618
```

Figure 5-45. *Output data when executing a "scissors" gesture*

```
16.58618542899717
12.84692810776346
13.672851672721777
11.591463364483616
12.502871018025076
13.116153410465017
14.751265678288632
11.154542514320497
8.140579542089768
8.58151598263089
9.735567351660848
8.253672620372754
7.993735399951447
9.217670689773172
10.561947833336376
8.279970537461281
9.305179645444014
4.950082042127633
7.91517907373759
10.4731313234945
9.089622895534717
13.941180389809233
12.780371313666592
11.551242460390995
7.5509458375570375
6.414258162925421
8.559458749292276
```

Figure 5-46. *Output data when executing another gesture*

We can see that when we do the "scissors" gesture, the value of the diffFingersX variable is much higher than when the two fingers are close together.

Looking at this data, we could decide that our threshold could be 100. If the value of diffFingersX is more than 100 and the ring and little fingers are folded, the likelihood of the gesture being "scissors" is very high.

So, altogether, we could check this gesture with the following code sample.

Listing 5-39. Detect "scissors" gesture

```
let ringBase = predictions[0].annotations.ringFinger[0][1];
let ringTip = predictions[0].annotations.ringFinger[3][1];
let pinkyBase = predictions[0].annotations.pinky[0][1];
let pinkyTip = predictions[0].annotations.pinky[3][1];
```

```
let ringExtended = ringBase > ringTip ? true : false;
let pinkyExtended = pinkyBase > pinkyTip ? true : false;

let indexTipX = predictions[0].annotations.indexFinger[3][0];
let middleTipX = predictions[0].annotations.middleFinger[3][0];

let diffFingersX =
      indexTipX > middleTipX ? indexTipX - middleTipX :
middleTipX - indexTipX;

if (diffFingersX > 100 && !ringExtended && !pinkyExtended) {
  console.log("scissors gesture!");
}
```

Figure 5-47. *Screenshot of "scissors" gesture detection working*

Now that we wrote the logic to detect the gestures separately, let's put it all together.

217

Listing 5-40. Logic for detecting all gestures

```
let indexBase = predictions[0].annotations.indexFinger[0][1];
let indexTip = predictions[0].annotations.indexFinger[3][1];
let thumbBase = predictions[0].annotations.thumb[0][1];
let thumbTip = predictions[0].annotations.thumb[3][1];
let middleBase = predictions[0].annotations.middleFinger[0][1];
let middleTip = predictions[0].annotations.middleFinger[3][1];
let ringBase = predictions[0].annotations.ringFinger[0][1];
let ringTip = predictions[0].annotations.ringFinger[3][1];
let pinkyBase = predictions[0].annotations.pinky[0][1];
let pinkyTip = predictions[0].annotations.pinky[3][1];

let indexExtended = indexBase > indexTip ? true : false;
let thumbExtended = thumbBase > thumbTip ? true : false;
let middleExtended = middleBase > middleTip ? true : false;
let ringExtended = ringBase > ringTip ? true : false;
let pinkyExtended = pinkyBase > pinkyTip ? true : false;

if (
    indexExtended &&
    thumbExtended &&
    middleExtended &&
    ringExtended &&
    pinkyExtended
) {
  console.log("paper gesture!");
}

/* Rock gesture */
if (!indexExtended && !middleExtended && !ringExtended &&
!pinkyExtended) {
    console.log("rock gesture!");
}
```

```
/* Scissors gesture */
let indexTipX = predictions[0].annotations.indexFinger[3][0];
let middleTipX = predictions[0].annotations.middleFinger[3][0];

let diffFingersX =
     indexTipX > middleTipX ? indexTipX - middleTipX :
     middleTipX - indexTipX;

if (diffFingersX > 100 && !ringExtended && !pinkyExtended) {
  console.log("scissors gesture!");
}
```

If everything works properly, you should see the correct message being logged in the console when you do each gesture!

Once you have verified that the logic works, you can move on from using console.log and use this to build a game or use these gestures as a controller for your interface, and so on.

The most important thing is to understand how the model works, get familiar with building logic using coordinates so you can explore the opportunities, and be conscious of some of the limits.

5.2.3 PoseNet

Finally, the last body tracking model we are going to talk about is called PoseNet.

PoseNet is a pose detection model that can estimate a single pose or multiple poses in an image or video.

Similarly to the Facemesh and Handpose models, PoseNet tracks the position of keypoints in a user's body.

The following is an example of these key points visualized.

Figure 5-48. *Visualization of the keypoints detected by PoseNet. Source: https://github.com/tensorflow/tfjs-models/tree/ master/posenet*

This body tracking model can detect 17 keypoints and their 2D coordinates, indexed by part ID.

Id	Part
0	nose
1	leftEye
2	rightEye
3	leftEar
4	rightEar
5	leftShoulder
6	rightShoulder
7	leftElbow
8	rightElbow
9	leftWrist
10	rightWrist
11	leftHip
12	rightHip
13	leftKnee
14	rightKnee
15	leftAnkle
16	rightAnkle

Figure 5-49. *List of keypoints and their ID. Source:* `https://github.com/tensorflow/tfjs-models/tree/master/posenet`

Even though this model is also specialized in tracking a person's body using the webcam feed, using it in your code is a little bit different from the two models we covered in the previous sections.

Importing and loading the model

Importing and loading the model follows the same standard as most of the code samples in this book.

Listing 5-41. Import TensorFlow.js and the PoseNet model in HTML

```
<script src="https://cdn.jsdelivr.net/npm/@tensorflow/tfjs"></
script>
<script src="https://cdn.jsdelivr.net/npm/@tensorflow-models/
posenet"></script>
```

Listing 5-42. Loading the model in JavaScript

```
const net = await posenet.load();
```

This default way of loading PoseNet uses a faster and smaller model based on the MobileNetV1 architecture. The trade-off for speed is a lower accuracy.

If you want to expcriment with the parameters, you can also load it this way.

Listing 5-43. Alternative ways of loading the model

```
const net = await posenet.load({
  architecture: 'MobileNetV1',
  outputStride: 16,
  inputResolution: { width: 640, height: 480 },
  multiplier: 0.75
});
```

If you want to try the second configuration available, you can indicate that you'd like to use the other model based on the ResNet50 architecture that has better accuracy but is a larger model, so will take more time to load.

Listing 5-44. Loading the model using the ResNet50 architecture

```
const net = await posenet.load({
  architecture: 'ResNet50',
  outputStride: 32,
  inputResolution: { width: 257, height: 200 },
  quantBytes: 2
});
```

If you feel a bit confused by the different parameters, don't worry, as you get started, using the default ones provided is completely fine. If you want to learn more about them, you can find more information in the official TensorFlow documentation.

Once the model is loaded, you can focus on predicting poses.

Predictions

To get predictions from the model, you mainly need to call the estimateSinglePose method on the model.

Listing 5-45. Predicting single poses

```
const pose = await net.estimateSinglePose(image, {
  flipHorizontal: false
});
```

The image parameter can either be some imageData, an HTML image element, an HTML canvas element, or an HTML video element. It represents the input image you want to get predictions on.

The flipHorizontal parameter indicates if you would like to flip/ mirror the pose horizontally. By default, its value is set to false.

If you are using videos, it should be set to true if the video is by default flipped horizontally (e.g., when using a webcam).

The preceding code sample will set the variable pose to a single pose object that will contain a confidence score and an array of keypoints detected, with their 2D coordinates, the name of the body part, and a probability score.

The following is an example of the object that will be returned.

Listing 5-46. Complete object returned as predictions

```
{
  "score": 0.32371445304906,
  "keypoints": [
    {
      "position": {
         "y": 76.291801452637,
         "x": 253.36747741699
      },
      "part": "nose",
      "score": 0.99539834260941
    },
    {
      "position": {
         "y": 71.10383605957,
         "x": 253.54365539551
      },
      "part": "leftEye",
      "score": 0.98781454563141
    },
```

```
{
  "position": {
    "y": 71.839515686035,
    "x": 246.00454711914
  },
  "part": "rightEye",
  "score": 0.99528175592422
},
{
  "position": {
    "y": 72.848854064941,
    "x": 263.08151245117
  },
  "part": "leftEar",
  "score": 0.84029853343964
},
{
  "position": {
    "y": 79.956565856934,
    "x": 234.26812744141
  },
  "part": "rightEar",
  "score": 0.92544466257095
},
{
  "position": {
    "y": 98.34538269043,
    "x": 399.64068603516
  },
  "part": "leftShoulder",
  "score": 0.99559044837952
},
```

```
{
  "position": {
    "y": 95.082359313965,
    "x": 458.21868896484
  },
  "part": "rightShoulder",
  "score": 0.99583911895752
},
{
  "position": {
    "y": 94.626205444336,
    "x": 163.94561767578
  },
  "part": "leftElbow",
  "score": 0.9518963098526
},
{
  "position": {
    "y": 150.2349395752,
    "x": 245.06030273438
  },
  "part": "rightElbow",
  "score": 0.98052614927292
},
{
  "position": {
    "y": 113.9603729248,
    "x": 393.19735717773
  },
  "part": "leftWrist",
  "score": 0.94009721279144
},
```

```
{
  "position": {
    "y": 186.47859191895,
    "x": 257.98034667969
  },
  "part": "rightWrist",
  "score": 0.98029226064682
},
{
  "position": {
    "y": 208.5266418457,
    "x": 284.46710205078
  },
  "part": "leftHip",
  "score": 0.97870296239853
},
{
  "position": {
    "y": 209.9910736084,
    "x": 243.31219482422
  },
  "part": "rightHip",
  "score": 0.97424703836441
},
{
  "position": {
    "y": 281.61965942383,
    "x": 310.93188476562
  },
  "part": "leftKnee",
  "score": 0.98368924856186
},
```

```
{
  "position": {
    "y": 282.80120849609,
    "x": 203.81164550781
  },
  "part": "rightKnee",
  "score": 0.96947449445724
},
{
  "position": {
    "y": 360.62716674805,
    "x": 292.21047973633
  },
  "part": "leftAnkle",
  "score": 0.8883239030838
},
{
  "position": {
    "y": 347.41177368164,
    "x": 203.88229370117
  },
  "part": "rightAnkle",
  "score": 0.8255187869072
}
  ]
}
```

If you would like to detect multiple poses, if you expect an image or video to contain multiple people, you can change the method called to be as follows.

Listing 5-47. Predicting multiple poses

```
const poses = await net.estimateMultiplePoses(image, {
  flipHorizontal: false,
  maxDetections: 5,
  scoreThreshold: 0.5,
  nmsRadius: 20
});
```

We can see that some additional parameters are passed in.

- **maxDetections** indicates the maximum number of poses we'd like to detect. The value 5 is the default but you can change it to more or less.

- **scoreThreshold** indicates that you only want instances to be returned if the score value at the root of the object is higher than the value set. 0.5 is the default value.

- **nmsRadius** stands for nonmaximum suppression and indicates the amount of pixels that should separate multiple poses detected. The value needs to be strictly positive and defaults to 20.

Using this method will set the value of the variable poses to an array of pose objects, like the following.

Listing 5-48. Output array when detecting multiple poses

```
[
  // Pose 1
  {
    // Pose score
    "score": 0.42985695206067,
    "keypoints": [
```

```
    {
      "position": {
        "x": 126.09371757507,
        "y": 97.861720561981
      },
      "part": "nose",
      "score": 0.99710708856583
    },
    {
      "position": {
        "x": 132.53466176987,
        "y": 86.429876804352
      },
      "part": "leftEye",
      "score": 0.99919074773788
    },
    ...
  ],
},
// Pose 2
{

  // Pose score
  "score": 0.13461434583673,
  "keypoints": [
    {
      "position": {
        "x": 116.58444058895,
        "y": 99.772533416748
      },
      "part": "nose",
      "score": 0.0028593824245036
    }
```

```
    {
      "position": {
        "x": 133.49897611141,
        "y": 79.644590377808
      },
      "part": "leftEye",
      "score": 0.99919074773788
    },
    ...
  ],
  }
]
```

Full code sample

Altogether, the code sample to set up the prediction of poses in an image is as follows.

Listing 5-49. HTML code to detect poses in an image

```
<html lang="en">
  <head>
    <meta charset="UTF-8" />
    <meta name="viewport" content="width=device-width, initial-
    scale=1.0" />
    <title>PoseNet</title>
  </head>
  <body>
    <!-- you can replace the path to the asset with any you'd
    like -->
    <img src="image-pose.jpg" alt="" />
    <script src="https://cdn.jsdelivr.net/npm/@tensorflow/
    tfjs"></script>
```

```
    <script src="https://cdn.jsdelivr.net/npm/@tensorflow-
    models/posenet"></script>
    <script src="index.js"></script>
  </body>
</html>
```

Listing 5-50. JavaScript code

```
const imageElement = document.getElementsByTagName("img")[0];

posenet
  .load()
  .then(function (net) {
    const pose = net.estimateSinglePose(imageElement, {
      flipHorizontal: true,
    });
    return pose;
  })
  .then(function (pose) {
    console.log(pose);
  })
  .catch((err) => console.log(err));
```

For a video from the webcam feed, the code should be as follows.

Listing 5-51. HTML code to detect poses in a video

```
<html lang="en">
  <head>
    <meta charset="UTF-8" />
    <meta name="viewport" content="width=device-width,
    initial-scale=1.0" />
    <title>PoseNet</title>
  </head>
```

```
<body>
  <video></video>
  <script src="https://cdn.jsdelivr.net/npm/@tensorflow/
  tfjs"></script>
  <script src="https://cdn.jsdelivr.net/npm/@tensorflow-
  models/posenet"></script>
  <script src="index.js"></script>
</body>
</html>
```

Listing 5-52. JavaScript code to detect poses in a video from the webcam

```
let video;
let model;

const init = async () => {
  video = await loadVideo();
  model = await posenet.load();
  main();
};

const loadVideo = async () => {
  const video = await setupCamera();
  video.play();
  return video;
};

const setupCamera = async () => {
  if (!navigator.mediaDevices || !navigator.mediaDevices.
  getUserMedia) {
    throw new Error(
```

```
      "Browser API navigator.mediaDevices.getUserMedia not
      available"
    );
  }

  video = document.querySelector("video");
  video.width = window.innerWidth;
  video.height = window.innerHeight;

  const stream = await navigator.mediaDevices.getUserMedia({
    audio: false,
    video: {
      facingMode: "user",
      width: window.innerWidth,
      height: window.innerHeight,
    },
  });
  video.srcObject = stream;

  return new Promise(
    (resolve) => (video.onloadedmetadata = () =>
    resolve(video))
  );
};

init();

const main = () => {
  const pose = model
    .estimateSinglePose(video, {
      flipHorizontal: true,
    })
```

```
    .then((pose) => {
      console.log(pose);
    });

  requestAnimationFrame(main);
};
```

Visualizing keypoints

So far, we've mainly used console.log to be able to see the results coming back from the model. However, you might want to visualize them on the page to make sure that the body tracking is working and that the keypoints are placed in the right position.

To do this, we are going to use the Canvas API.

We need to start by adding a HTML canvas element to the HTML file. Then, we can create a function that will access this element and its context, detect the poses, and draw the keypoints.

Accessing the canvas element and its context is done with the following lines.

Listing 5-53. Accessing the canvas element

```
const canvas = document.getElementById("output");
const ctx = canvas.getContext("2d");
canvas.width = window.innerWidth;
canvas.height = window.innerHeight;
```

Then, we can create a function that will call the estimateSinglePose method to start the detection, draw the video on the canvas, and loop through the keypoints found to render them on the canvas element.

Listing 5-54. Start the detection, draw the webcam feed on a canvas element, and render the keypoints

```
async function poseDetectionFrame() {
    const pose = await net.estimateSinglePose(video, {
      flipHorizontal: true
    });

    ctx.clearRect(0, 0, videoWidth, videoHeight);
    ctx.save();
    ctx.scale(-1, 1);
    ctx.translate(-videoWidth, 0);
    ctx.drawImage(video, 0, 0, window.innerWidth, window.
    innerHeight);
    ctx.restore();

    drawKeypoints(pose.keypoints, 0.5, ctx);
    drawSkeleton(pose.keypoints, 0.5, ctx);

    requestAnimationFrame(poseDetectionFrame);
}
```

The drawKeypoints and drawSkeleton functions use some of the Canvas API methods to draw circles and lines at the coordinates of the keypoints detected.

Listing 5-55. Some helper functions to draw the keypoints onto the canvas element

```
const color = "aqua";
const lineWidth = 2;

const toTuple = ({ y, x }) => [y, x];

function drawPoint(ctx, y, x, r, color) {
  ctx.beginPath();
```

```
  ctx.arc(x, y, r, 0, 2 * Math.PI);
  ctx.fillStyle = color;
  ctx.fill();
}

function drawSegment([ay, ax], [by, bx], color, scale, ctx) {
  ctx.beginPath();
  ctx.moveTo(ax * scale, ay * scale);
  ctx.lineTo(bx * scale, by * scale);
  ctx.lineWidth = lineWidth;
  ctx.strokeStyle = color;
  ctx.stroke();
}

function drawSkeleton(keypoints, minConfidence, ctx, scale = 1)
{
  const adjacentKeyPoints = posenet.getAdjacentKeyPoints(
    keypoints,
    minConfidence
  );

  adjacentKeyPoints.forEach((keypoints) => {
    drawSegment(
      toTuple(keypoints[0].position),
      toTuple(keypoints[1].position),
      color,
      scale,
      ctx
    );
  });
}
```

```
function drawKeypoints(keypoints, minConfidence, ctx, scale = 1) {
  for (let i = 0; i < keypoints.length; i++) {
    const keypoint = keypoints[i];

    if (keypoint.score < minConfidence) {
      continue;
    }

    const { y, x } = keypoint.position;
    drawPoint(ctx, y * scale, x * scale, 3, color);
  }
}
```

The poseDetectionFrame function should be called once the video and model are loaded.

Altogether, the full code sample should look like the following.

Listing 5-56. Complete HTML code to visualize keypoints

```
<html lang="en">
  <head>
    <meta charset="UTF-8" />
    <meta name="viewport" content="width=device-width, initial-
    scale=1.0" />
    <title>PoseNet</title>
  </head>
  <body>
    <video id="video"></video>
    <canvas id="output" />
    <script src="https://cdn.jsdelivr.net/npm/@tensorflow/
    tfjs"></script>
    <script src="https://cdn.jsdelivr.net/npm/@tensorflow-
    models/posenet"></script>
```

```
    <script src="utils.js" type="module"></script>
    <script src="index.js" type="module"></script>
  </body>
</html>
```

Listing 5-57. JavaScript code to visualize keypoints in index.js

```
import { drawKeypoints, drawSkeleton } from "./utils.js";

const videoWidth = window.innerWidth;
const videoHeight = window.innerHeight;

async function setupCamera() {
  if (!navigator.mediaDevices || !navigator.mediaDevices.
  getUserMedia) {
    throw new Error(
      "Browser API navigator.mediaDevices.getUserMedia not
      available"
    );
  }

  const video = document.getElementById("video");
  video.width = videoWidth;
  video.height = videoHeight;

  const stream = await navigator.mediaDevices.getUserMedia({
    audio: false,
    video: {
      facingMode: "user",
      width: videoWidth,
      height: videoHeight,
    },
  });
  video.srcObject = stream;
```

```
  return new Promise((resolve) => {
    video.onloadedmetadata = () => {
      resolve(video);
    };
  });
}

async function loadVideo() {
  const video = await setupCamera();
  video.play();

  return video;
}

function detectPoseInRealTime(video, net) {
  const canvas = document.getElementById("output");
  const ctx = canvas.getContext("2d");

  const flipPoseHorizontal = true;

  canvas.width = videoWidth;
  canvas.height = videoHeight;

  async function poseDetectionFrame() {
    let minPoseConfidence;
    let minPartConfidence;

    const pose = await net.estimateSinglePose(video, {
      flipHorizontal: flipPoseHorizontal,
    });

    minPoseConfidence = 0.1;
    minPartConfidence = 0.5;

    ctx.clearRect(0, 0, videoWidth, videoHeight);
```

```
    ctx.save();
    ctx.scale(-1, 1);
    ctx.translate(-videoWidth, 0);
    ctx.drawImage(video, 0, 0, videoWidth, videoHeight);
    ctx.restore();

    drawKeypoints(pose.keypoints, minPartConfidence, ctx);
    drawSkeleton(pose.keypoints, minPartConfidence, ctx);

    requestAnimationFrame(poseDetectionFrame);
  }

  poseDetectionFrame();
}

let net;
export async function init() {
  net = await posenet.load();

  let video;

  try {
    video = await loadVideo();
  } catch (e) {
    throw e;
  }
  detectPoseInRealTime(video, net);
}

navigator.getUserMedia =
  navigator.getUserMedia ||
  navigator.webkitGetUserMedia ||
  navigator.mozGetUserMedia;
init();
```

Listing 5-58. JavaScript code to visualize keypoints in utils.js

```javascript
const color = "aqua";
const lineWidth = 2;

function toTuple({ y, x }) {
  return [y, x];
}

export function drawPoint(ctx, y, x, r, color) {
  ctx.beginPath();
  ctx.arc(x, y, r, 0, 2 * Math.PI);
  ctx.fillStyle = color;
  ctx.fill();
}

export function drawSegment([ay, ax], [by, bx], color, scale,
ctx) {
  ctx.beginPath();
  ctx.moveTo(ax * scale, ay * scale);
  ctx.lineTo(bx * scale, by * scale);
  ctx.lineWidth = lineWidth;
  ctx.strokeStyle = color;
  ctx.stroke();
}

export function drawSkeleton(keypoints, minConfidence, ctx,
scale = 1) {
  const adjacentKeyPoints = posenet.getAdjacentKeyPoints(
    keypoints,
    minConfidence
  );
```

```
  adjacentKeyPoints.forEach((keypoints) => {
    drawSegment(
      toTuple(keypoints[0].position),
      toTuple(keypoints[1].position),
      color,
      scale,
      ctx
    );
  });
}

export function drawKeypoints(keypoints, minConfidence, ctx,
scale = 1) {
  for (let i = 0; i < keypoints.length; i++) {
    const keypoint = keypoints[i];

    if (keypoint.score < minConfidence) {
      continue;
    }

    const { y, x } = keypoint.position;
    drawPoint(ctx, y * scale, x * scale, 3, color);
  }
}
```

The output of this code should visualize the keypoints like the following.

Figure 5-50. *Output of the complete code sample*

Figure 5-51. *Output of the complete code sample*

Now that we have gone through the code to detect poses, access coordinates for different parts of the body, and visualize them on a canvas, feel free to experiment with this data to create projects exploring new interactions.

5.3 Hardware data

For the last section of this chapter and the last part of the book that will contain code samples, we are going to look into something a bit more advanced and experimental. The next few pages will focus on using data generated by hardware and build a custom machine learning model to detect gestures.

Usually, when working with hardware, I use microcontrollers such as Arduino or Raspberry Pi; however, to make it more accessible to anyone reading this book that might not have access to such material, this next section is going to use another device that has built-in hardware components, your mobile phone!

This is assuming you possess a modern mobile phone with at least an accelerometer and gyroscope.

To have access to this data in JavaScript, we are going to use the Generic Sensor API.

This API is rather new and experimental and has browser support only in Chrome at the moment, so if you decide to write the following code samples, make sure to use Chrome as your browser.

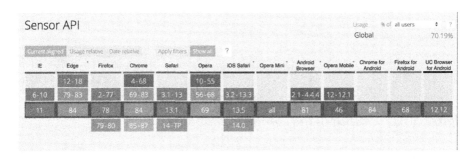

Figure 5-52. *Browser support for the Generic Sensor API. Source:*
`https://caniuse.com/#search=sensor%20api`

To build our gesture classifier, we are going to access and record data from the accelerometer and gyroscope present in your phone, save this data into files in your project, create a machine learning model, train it, and run predictions on new live data.

To be able to do this, we are going to need a little bit of Node.js, web sockets with socket.io, the Generic Sensor API, and TensorFlow.js.

If you are unfamiliar with some of these technologies, don't worry, I'm going to explain each part and provide code samples you should be able to follow.

5.3.1 Web Sensors API

As we are using hardware data in this section, the first thing we need to do is verify that we can access the correct data.

As said a little earlier, we need to record data from the gyroscope and accelerometer.

The gyroscope gives us details about the orientation of the device and its angular velocity, and the accelerometer focuses on giving us data about the acceleration.

Even though we could use only one of these sensors if we wanted, I believe that combining data of both gyroscope and accelerometer gives us more precise information about the motion and will be helpful for gesture recognition.

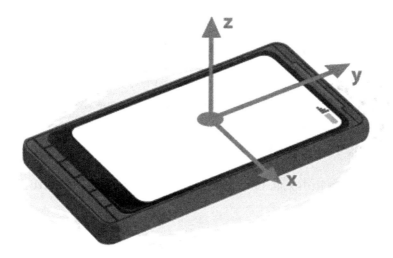

Figure 5-53. *Accelerometer axes on mobile phone. Source:*
https://developers.google.com/web/fundamentals/native-
hardware/device-orientation

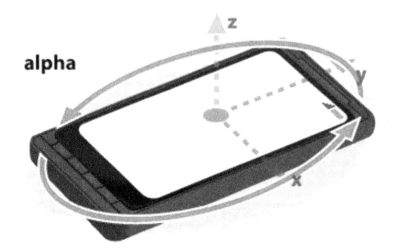

Figure 5-54. *Gyroscope axes on mobile phone. Source:* `https://www.sitepoint.com/using-device-orientation-html5/`

5.3.2 Accessing sensors data

To access the data using the Generic Sensor API, we need to start by declaring a few variables: one that will refer to the `requestAnimationFrame` statement so we can cancel it later on, and two others that will contain gyroscope and accelerometer data.

Listing 5-59. In index.js. Declaring variables to contain hardware data

```
let dataRequest;
let gyroscopeData = {
    x: '',
    y: '',
    z: ''
}
```

```
let accelerometerData = {
    x: '',
    y: '',
    z: ''
}
```

Then, to access the phone's sensors data, you will need to instantiate a new Gyroscope and Accelerometer interface, use the `reading` event listener to get the x, y, and z coordinates of the device's motion, and call the `start` method to start the tracking.

Listing 5-60. In index.js. Get accelerometer and gyroscope data

```
function initSensors() {
    let gyroscope = new Gyroscope({frequency: 60});

    gyroscope.addEventListener('reading', e => {
        gyroscopeData.x = gyroscope.x;
        gyroscopeData.y = gyroscope.y;
        gyroscopeData.z = gyroscope.z;
    });
    gyroscope.start();

    let accelerometer = new Accelerometer({frequency: 60});

    accelerometer.addEventListener('reading', e => {
        accelerometerData.x = accelerometer.x;
        accelerometerData.y = accelerometer.y;
        accelerometerData.z = accelerometer.z;
    });
    accelerometer.start();
}
```

Finally, as we are interested in recording data when we are executing a specific gesture, we need to call the preceding function only when the user is pressing on the mobile screen with the touchstart event. We also should cancel it on touchend.

Listing 5-61. In index.js. Use the touchstart event listener to start displaying data

```
function getData() {
  let data = {
    xAcc: accelerometerData.x,
    yAcc: accelerometerData.y,
    zAcc: accelerometerData.z,
    xGyro: gyroscopeData.x,
    yGyro: gyroscopeData.y,
    zGyro: gyroscopeData.z,
  };
  document.body.innerHTML = JSON.stringify(data);
  dataRequest = requestAnimationFrame(getData);
}

window.onload = function () {
  initSensors();

  document.body.addEventListener("touchstart", (e) => {
    getData();
  });
  document.body.addEventListener("touchend", (e) => {
    cancelAnimationFrame(dataRequest);
  });
};
```

At this point, if you want to check the output of this code, you will need to visit the page on your mobile phone using a tool like ngrok, for example, to create a tunnel to your localhost.

What you should see is the live accelerometer and gyroscope data displayed on the screen when you press it, and when you release it, the data should not update anymore.

At this point, we display the data on the page so we can double check that everything is working as expected.

However, what we really need is to store this data in file when we record gestures. For this, we are going to need web sockets to send the data from the front-end to a back-end server that will be in charge of writing the data to files in our application folder.

5.3.3 Setting up web sockets

To set up web sockets, we are going to use socket.io.

So far, in all previous examples, we only worked with HTML and JavaScript files without any back end.

If you have never written any Node.js before, you will need to install it as well as **npm** or **yarn** to be able to install packages.

Once you have these two tools set up, at the root of your project folder, in your terminal, write `npm init` to generate a package.json file that will contain some details about the project.

Once your package.json file is generated, in your terminal, write `npm install socket.io` to install the package.

Once this is done, add the following script tag in your HTML file.

Listing 5-62. Import the socket.io script in the HTML file

```
<script type="text/javascript" src="./../socket.io/socket.
io.js"></script>
```

Now, you should be able to use socket.io in the front end. In your
JavaScript file, start by instantiating it with `const socket = io()`.

If you have any issue with setting up the package, feel free to refer to
the official documentation.

Then, in our event listener for `touchstart`, we can use socket.io to
send data to the server with the following data.

Listing 5-63. Send motion data via web sockets

```
socket.emit("motion data", `${accelerometerData.x}
${accelerometerData.y} ${accelerometerData.z}
${gyroscopeData.x} ${gyroscopeData.y} ${gyroscopeData.z}`);
```

We are sending the motion data as a string as we want to write these
values down into files.

On `touchend`, we need to send another event indicating that we want
to stop the emission of data with `socket.emit('end motion data')`.

Altogether, our first JavaScript file should look like the following.

Listing 5-64. Complete JavaScript code in the index.js file

```
const socket = io();
let gyroscopeData = {
  x: "",
  y: "",
  z: "",
};
let accelerometerData = {
  x: "",
  y: "",
  z: "",
};
```

```
let dataRequest;

function initSensors() {
  let gyroscope = new Gyroscope({ frequency: 60 });

  gyroscope.addEventListener("reading", (e) => {
    gyroscopeData.x = gyroscope.x;
    gyroscopeData.y = gyroscope.y;
    gyroscopeData.z = gyroscope.z;
  });
  gyroscope.start();

  let accelerometer = new Accelerometer({ frequency: 60 });

  accelerometer.addEventListener("reading", (e) => {
    accelerometerData.x = accelerometer.x;
    accelerometerData.y = accelerometer.y;
    accelerometerData.z = accelerometer.z;
  });
  accelerometer.start();
}

function getData() {
  dataRequest = requestAnimationFrame(getData);
  socket.emit(
    "motion data",
    `${accelerometerData.x} ${accelerometerData.y}
    ${accelerometerData.z} ${gyroscopeData.x}
    ${gyroscopeData.y} ${gyroscopeData.z}`
  );
}
```

```
window.onload = function () {
  initSensors();

  document.body.addEventListener("touchstart", (e) => {
    getData();
  });
  document.body.addEventListener("touchend", (e) => {
    socket.emit("end motion data");
    cancelAnimationFrame(dataRequest);
  });
};
```

Now, let's implement the server side of this project to serve our front-end files, receive the data, and store it into text files.

First, we need to create a new JavaScript file. I personally named it server.js.

To serve our front-end files, we are going to use the express npm package. To install it, type npm install express --save in your terminal.

Once installed, write the following code to create a '/record' route that will serve our index.html file.

Listing 5-65. Initial setup of the server.js file

```
const express = require("express");
const app = express();
var http = require("http").createServer(app);

app.use("/record", express.static(__dirname + '/'));

http.listen(process.env.PORT || 3000);
```

You should be able to type node server.js in your terminal, visit http://localhost:3000/record in your browser, and it should serve the index.html file we created previously.

Now, let's test our web sockets connection by requiring the socket.io package and write the back-end code that will receive messages from the front end.

At the top of the server.js file, require the package with `const io = require('socket.io')(http)`.

Then, set up the connection and listen to events with the following data.

Listing 5-66. In server.js. Web sockets connection

```
io.on("connection", function (socket) {
  socket.on("motion data", function (data) {
    console.log(data);
  });

  socket.on("end motion data", function () {
    console.log('end');
  });
});
```

Now, restart the server, visit the page on '/record' on your mobile, and you should see motion data logged in your terminal when you touch your mobile's screen.

If you don't see anything, **double check that your page is served using https**.

At this point, we know that the web sockets connection is properly set up, and the following step is to save this data into files in our application so we'll be able to use it to train a machine learning algorithm.

To save files, we are going to use the Node.js File System module, so we need to start by requiring it with `const fs = require('fs');`.

Then, we are going to write some code that will be able to handle arguments passed when starting the server, so we can easily record new samples.

For example, if we want to record three gestures, one performing the letter A in the air, the second the letter B, and the third the letter C, we want to be able to type node `server.js letterA 1` to indicate that we are currently recording data for the letter A gesture (`letterA` parameter) and that this is the first sample (the 1 parameter).

The following code will handle these two arguments, store them in variables, and use them to name the new file created.

Listing 5-67. In server.js. Code to handle arguments passed in to generate file names dynamically

```
let stream;
let sampleNumber;
let gestureType;
let previousSampleNumber;

process.argv.forEach(function (val, index, array) {
  gestureType = array[2];
  sampleNumber = parseInt(array[3]);
  previousSampleNumber = sampleNumber;
  stream = fs.createWriteStream(
    `data/sample_${gestureType}_${sampleNumber}.txt`,
    { flags: "a" }
  );
});
```

Now, when starting the server, you will need to pass these two arguments (gesture type and sample number).

To actually write the data from the front end to these files, we need to write the following lines of code.

Listing 5-68. In server.js. Code to create a file and stream when receiving data

```
socket.on("motion data", function (data) {
    /* This following line allows us to record new files
    without having to start/stop the server. On motion end,
    we increment the sampleNumber variable so when receiving
    new data, we deduce it is related to a new gesture and
    create a file with the correct sample number. */
    if (sampleNumber !== previousSampleNumber) {
      stream = fs.createWriteStream(
        `./data/sample_${gestureType}_${sampleNumber}.txt`,
        { flags: "a" }
      );
    }
    stream.write(`${data}\r\n`);
});

socket.on("end motion data", function () {
    stream.end();
    sampleNumber += 1;
});
```

We also close the stream when receiving the "end motion data" event so we stop writing motion data when the user has stopped touching their phone's screen, as this means they've stopped executing the gesture we want to record.

To test this setup, start by creating an empty folder in your application called 'data', then type node server.js letterA 1 in your terminal, visit back the web page on your mobile, and execute the gesture of the letter A in the air while pressing the screen, and when releasing, you should see a new file named sample_letterA_1.text in the data folder, and it should contain gesture data!

At this stage, we are able to get accelerometer and gyroscope data, send it to our server using web sockets, and save it into files in our application.

Listing 5-69. Complete code sample in the server.js file

```
const express = require("express");
const app = express();
const http = require("http").createServer(app);
const io = require('socket.io')(http);
const fs = require('fs');
let stream;
let sampleNumber;
let gestureType;
let previousSampleNumber;

app.use("/record", express.static(__dirname + '/'));

process.argv.forEach(function (val, index, array) {
  gestureType = array[2];
  sampleNumber = parseInt(array[3]);
  previousSampleNumber = sampleNumber;
  stream = fs.createWriteStream(
    `data/sample_${gestureType}_${sampleNumber}.txt`,
    { flags: "a" }
  );
});

io.on("connection", function (socket) {
  socket.on("motion data", function (data) {
    if (sampleNumber !== previousSampleNumber) {
      stream = fs.createWriteStream(
        `./data/sample_${gestureType}_${sampleNumber}.txt`,
```

```
      { flags: "a" }
    );
  }
  stream.write(`${data}\r\n`);
});

  socket.on("end motion data", function () {
    stream.end();
    sampleNumber += 1;
  });
});

http.listen(process.env.PORT || 3000);
```

Before moving on to writing the code responsible for formatting our data and creating the machine learning model, make sure to record a few samples of data for each of our three gestures; the more, the better, but I would advise to **record at least 20 samples per gesture**.

5.3.4 Data processing

For this section, I would advise to create a new JavaScript file. I personally called it `train.js`.

In this file, we are going to read through the text files we recorded in the previous step, transform the data from strings to tensors, and create and train our model. Some of the following code samples are not directly related to TensorFlow.js (reading folders and files, and formatting the data into multidimensional arrays), so I will not dive into them too much.

The first step here is to go through our data folder, get the data for each sample and gesture, and organize it into arrays of features and labels.

For this, I used the line-reader npm package, so we need to install it using `npm install line-reader`.

We also need to install TensorFlow with `npm install @tensorflow/tfjs-node`.

Then, I created two functions `readDir` and `readFile` to loop through all the files in the data folder and for each file, loop through each line, transform strings into numbers, and return an object containing the label and features for that gesture.

Listing 5-70. In train.js. Loop through files to transform raw data into objects of features and labels

```
const lineReader = require("line-reader");
var fs = require("fs");
const tf = require("@tensorflow/tfjs-node");

const gestureClasses = ["letterA", "letterB", "letterC"];
let numClasses = gestureClasses.length;

let numSamplesPerGesture = 20; // the number of times you
recorded each gesture.
let totalNumDataFiles = numSamplesPerGesture * numClasses;
let numPointsOfData = 6; // x, y, and z for both accelerometer
and gyroscope
let numLinesPerFile = 100; // Files might have a different
amount of lines so we need a value to truncate and make sure
all our samples have the same length.
let totalNumDataPerFile = numPointsOfData * numLinesPerFile;

function readFile(file) {
  let allFileData = [];

  return new Promise((resolve, reject) => {
    fs.readFile(`data/${file}`, "utf8", (err, data) => {
      if (err) {
        reject(err);
      } else {
```

```
    lineReader.eachLine(`data/${file}`, function (line) {
      // Turn each line into an array of floats.
      let dataArray = line
        .split(" ")
        .map((arrayItem) => parseFloat(arrayItem));
      allFileData.push(...dataArray);
      let concatArray = [...allFileData];

      if (concatArray.length === totalNumDataPerFile) {
        // Get the label from the filename
        let label = file.split("_")[1];
        let labelIndex = gestureClasses.indexOf(label);
        // Return an object with data as features and the
        label index
        resolve({ features: concatArray, label: labelIndex });
      }
    });
  }
    });
  });
}

const readDir = () =>
  new Promise((resolve, reject) =>
    fs.readdir(`data/`, "utf8", (err, data) =>
      err ? reject(err) : resolve(data)
    )
  );

(async () => {
  const filenames = await readDir();
  let allData = [];
```

```
filenames.map(async (file) => {
  let originalContent = await readFile(file);
  allData.push(originalContent);
  if (allData.length === totalNumDataFiles) {
    console.log(allData);
  }
});
})();
```

I am not going to dive deeper into the preceding code sample, but I added some inline comments to help.

If you run this code using node train.js, you should get some output similar to the following figure.

```
{
  features: [
      -4.1000000000000005,                    9,     5.6000000000000005,
    -0.024434609527920613,   1.5707963267948966,  -0.019198621771937624,
                     -5.2,                 11.5,     3.8000000000000003,
      0.31066860685499065,   1.5236724369910497,    -0.2844886680750757,
                     -5.2,                 11.5,     3.8000000000000003,
      0.31066860685499065,   1.5236724369910497,    -0.2844886680750757,
                     -7.2,                   12,                    0.2,
       0.3769911184307752,  0.10646508437165411,    -0.5201081170943103,
                       -9,                 10.9,                    5.2,
      0.34732052114687156,  -1.1798425743481669,    -0.5393067388662478,
                    -12.5,                  9.9,                      9,
       0.6719517620178169,  -0.8587019919812101,    -0.3298672286269283,
                    -12.5,                  9.9,                      9,
       0.6719517620178169,  -0.8587019919812101,    -0.3298672286269283,
                    -12.5,                  9.9,                      9,
        1.090830782496456,  0.012217304763960306,  -0.10821041362364843,
      -14.100000000000001,                  6.9,                    5.2,
        1.085594794740473,   0.5602506898901798,     0.4537856055185257,
      -14.100000000000001,                  6.9,                    5.2,
        1.085594794740473,   0.5602506898901798,     0.4537856055185257,
      -14.100000000000001,                  6.9,                    5.2,
        1.085594794740473,   0.5602506898901798,     0.4537856055185257,
      -14.700000000000001,   5.300000000000001,     4.6000000000000005,
       0.9354964790689606,   0.7609635538695277,     0.9145525280450287,
      -14.700000000000001,   5.300000000000001,     4.6000000000000005,
       0.9354964790689606,   0.7609635538695277,     0.9145525280450287,
      -13.200000000000001,                  2.6,                    3.6,
       0.9058258817850571,   0.7766715171374766,     1.4835298641951802,
      -13.200000000000001,                  2.6,                    3.6,
       0.8237954069413236,   0.9459684545809266,     2.0629791758572975,
      -13.200000000000001,                  2.6,                    3.6,
       0.8237954069413236,   0.9459684545809266,     2.0629791758572975,
                     -9.1,   1.7000000000000002,     1.4000000000000001,
       0.5375614096142535,
    ... 500 more items
  ],
  label: 2
}
```

Figure 5-55. *Sample output of formatted data*

At this point, our variable `allData` holds all features and labels for each gesture sample, but we are not done yet. Before feeding this data to a machine learning algorithm, we need to transform it to tensors, the data type that TensorFlow.js works with.

The following code samples are going to be more complicated as we need to format the data further, create tensors, split them between a training set and a test set to validate our future predictions, and then generate the model.

I have added inline comments to attempt to explain each step.

So, where we wrote `console.log(allData)` in the preceding code, replace it with `format(allData)`, and the following is going to show the implementation of this function.

Listing 5-71. In train.js. Sorting and formatting the data

```
let justFeatures = [];
let justLabels = [];

const format = (allData) => {
  // Sort all data by label to get [{label: 0, features: ...},
     {label: 1, features: ...}];
  let sortedData = allData.sort((a, b) => (a.label > b.label ?
  1 : -1));
 // Tensorflow works with arrays and not objects so we need to
separate labels and tensors.
  sortedData.map((item) => {
    createMultidimentionalArrays(justLabels, item.label,
    item.label);
    createMultidimentionalArrays(justFeatures, item.label,
    item.features);
  });
};
```

```
function createMultidimentionalArrays(dataArray, index, item) {
  !dataArray[index] && dataArray.push([]);
  dataArray[index].push(item);
}
```

Running this should result in `justFeatures` and `justLabels` being multidimensional arrays containing features and labels indices, respectively.

For example, `justLabels` should look like [[0, 0, 0, 0, 0, 0, 0, 0, 0, 0, 0, 0, 0, 0, 0, 0, 0, 0, 0], [1, 1, 1, 1, 1, 1, 1, 1, 1, 1, 1, 1, 1, 1, 1, 1, 1, 1, 1, 1, 1], [2, 2, 2, 2, 2, 2, 2, 2, 2, 2, 2, 2, 2, 2, 2, 2, 2, 2, 2]].

Now that we are getting closer to a format TensorFlow can work with, we still need to transform these multidimensional arrays to tensors. To do this, let's start by creating a function called `transformToTensor`.

Listing 5-72. In train.js. Transforming multidimensional arrays into tensors

```
const [
    trainingFeatures,
    trainingLabels,
    testingFeatures,
    testingLabels,
] = transformToTensor(justFeatures, justLabels);

const transformToTensor = (features, labels) => {
  return tf.tidy(() => {
    // Preparing to split the dataset between training set and
    test set.
    const featureTrainings = [];
    const labelTrainings = [];
    const featureTests = [];
    const labelTests = [];
```

```
// For each gesture trained, convert the data to tensors
and store it between training set and test set.
for (let i = 0; i < gestureClasses.length; ++i) {
  const [
    featureTrain,
    labelTrain,
    featureTest,
    labelTest,
  ] = convertToTensors(features[i], labels[i], 0.2);
  featureTrainings.push(featureTrain);
  labelTrainings.push(labelTrain);
  featureTests.push(featureTest);
  labelTests.push(labelTest);
}

// Return all data concatenated
return [
  tf.concat(featureTrainings, 0),
  tf.concat(labelTrainings, 0),
  tf.concat(featureTests, 0),
  tf.concat(labelTests, 0),
];
});
};
```

The preceding code calls a function called convertToTensors so let's define it.

Listing 5-73. In train.js. Convert data to tensors

```
const convertToTensors = (featuresData, labelData, testSplit)
=> {
  if (featuresData.length !== labelData.length) {
    throw new Error(
      "features set and labels set have different numbers of
      examples"
    );
  }
  // Shuffle the data to avoid having a model that gets used to
  the order of the samples.
  const [shuffledFeatures, shuffledLabels] = shuffleData(
    featuresData,
    labelData
  );

  // Create the tensor
  const featuresTensor = tf.tensor2d(shuffledFeatures, [
    numSamplesPerGesture,
    totalNumDataPerFile,
  ]);

  // Create a 1D `tf.Tensor` to hold the labels, and convert
  the number label from the set {0, 1, 2} into one-hot encoding
  (e.g., 0 --> [1, 0, 0]).
  const labelsTensor = tf.oneHot(
    tf.tensor1d(shuffledLabels).toInt(),
    numClasses
  );
  // Split all this data into training set and test set and
  return it.
  return split(featuresTensor, labelsTensor, testSplit);
};
```

This function calls two other functions, `shuffleData` and `split`.

Listing 5-74. In train.js. Shuffle the data

```
const shuffleData = (features, labels) => {
  const indices = [...Array(numSamplesPerGesture).keys()];
  tf.util.shuffle(indices);

  const shuffledFeatures = [];
  const shuffledLabels = [];

  features.map((featuresArray, index) => {
    shuffledFeatures.push(features[indices[index]]);
    shuffledLabels.push(labels[indices[index]]);
  });

  return [shuffledFeatures, shuffledLabels];
};
```

Listing 5-75. In train.js. Split the data into training and test set

```
const split = (featuresTensor, labelsTensor, testSplit) => {
  // Split the data into a training set and a test set, based
    on `testSplit`.
  const numTestExamples = Math.round(numSamplesPerGesture *
  testSplit);
  const numTrainExamples = numSamplesPerGesture -
  numTestExamples;

  const trainingFeatures = featuresTensor.slice(
    [0, 0],
    [numTrainExamples, totalNumDataPerFile]
  );
```

```
const testingFeatures = featuresTensor.slice(
  [numTrainExamples, 0],
  [numTestExamples, totalNumDataPerFile]
);
const trainingLabels = labelsTensor.slice(
  [0, 0],
  [numTrainExamples, numClasses]
);

const testingLabels = labelsTensor.slice(
  [numTrainExamples, 0],
  [numTestExamples, numClasses]
);

return [trainingFeatures, trainingLabels, testingFeatures,
testingLabels];
};
```

At this point, if you add a console.log statement in the code to log the trainingFeatures variable in the format function, you should get a tensor as output.

Listing 5-76. Example of output tensor

```
Tensor {
  kept: false,
  isDisposedInternal: false,
  shape: [ 12, 600 ],
  dtype: 'float32',
  size: 7200,
  strides: [ 600 ],
  dataId: {},
```

```
  id: 70,
  rankType: '2',
  scopeId: 0
}
```

The values in the "shape" array will differ depending on how many samples of data you train and the number of lines per file.

Altogether, the code sample starting from the format function should look like the following.

Listing 5-77. In train.js. Full code sample for formatting the data

```
const format = (allData) => {
  let sortedData = allData.sort((a, b) => (a.label > b.label ?
  1 : -1));

  sortedData.map((item) => {
    createMultidimentionalArrays(justLabels, item.label, item.
    label);
    createMultidimentionalArrays(justFeatures, item.label,
    item.features);
  });

  const [
    trainingFeatures,
    trainingLabels,
    testingFeatures,
    testingLabels,
  ] = transformToTensor(justFeatures, justLabels);
};

function createMultidimentionalArrays(dataArray, index, item) {
  !dataArray[index] && dataArray.push([]);
  dataArray[index].push(item);
}
```

```
const transformToTensor = (features, labels) => {
  return tf.tidy(() => {
    const featureTrainings = [];
    const labelTrainings = [];
    const featureTests = [];
    const labelTests = [];
    for (let i = 0; i < gestureClasses.length; ++i) {
      const [
        featureTrain,
        labelTrain,
        featureTest,
        labelTest,
      ] = convertToTensors(features[i], labels[i], 0.2);
      featureTrainings.push(featureTrain);
      labelTrainings.push(labelTrain);
      featureTests.push(featureTest);
      labelTests.push(labelTest);
    }

    return [
      tf.concat(featureTrainings, 0),
      tf.concat(labelTrainings, 0),
      tf.concat(featureTests, 0),
      tf.concat(labelTests, 0),
    ];
  });
};

const convertToTensors = (featuresData, labelData, testSplit)
=> {
  if (featuresData.length !== labelData.length) {
    throw new Error(
```

```
      "features set and labels set have different numbers of
      examples"
    );
  }
  const [shuffledFeatures, shuffledLabels] = shuffleData(
    featuresData,
    labelData
  );
  const featuresTensor = tf.tensor2d(shuffledFeatures, [
    numSamplesPerGesture,
    totalNumDataPerFile,
  ]);
  const labelsTensor = tf.oneHot(
    tf.tensor1d(shuffledLabels).toInt(),
    numClasses
  );
  return split(featuresTensor, labelsTensor, testSplit);
};
const shuffleData = (features, labels) => {
  const indices = [...Array(numSamplesPerGesture).keys()];
  tf.util.shuffle(indices);

  const shuffledFeatures = [];
  const shuffledLabels = [];

  features.map((featuresArray, index) => {
    shuffledFeatures.push(features[indices[index]]);
    shuffledLabels.push(labels[indices[index]]);
  });

  return [shuffledFeatures, shuffledLabels];
};
```

```
const split = (featuresTensor, labelsTensor, testSplit) => {
  const numTestExamples = Math.round(numSamplesPerGesture *
  testSplit);
  const numTrainExamples = numSamplesPerGesture -
  numTestExamples;

  const trainingFeatures = featuresTensor.slice(
    [0, 0],
    [numTrainExamples, totalNumDataPerFile]
  );
  const testingFeatures = featuresTensor.slice(
    [numTrainExamples, 0],
    [numTestExamples, totalNumDataPerFile]
  );
  const trainingLabels = labelsTensor.slice(
    [0, 0],
    [numTrainExamples, numClasses]
  );

  const testingLabels = labelsTensor.slice(
    [numTrainExamples, 0],
    [numTestExamples, numClasses]
  );

  return [trainingFeatures, trainingLabels, testingFeatures,
  testingLabels];
};
```

It is a lot to take in if you are new to machine learning and TensorFlow.
js, but we are almost there. Our data is formatted and split between a
training set and a test set, so the last step is the creation of the model and
the training.

5.3.5 Creating and training the model

This part of the code is a bit arbitrary as there are multiple ways to create models and to pick values for parameters. However, you can copy the following code as a starting point and play around with different values later to see how they impact the accuracy of the model.

Listing 5-78. In train.js. Create, train, and save a model

```
const createModel = async (featureTrain, labelTrain,
featureTest, labelTest) => {
  const params = { learningRate: 0.1, epochs: 40 };
  // Instantiate a sequential model
  const model = tf.sequential();
  // Add a few layers
  model.add(
    tf.layers.dense({
      units: 10,
      activation: "sigmoid",
      inputShape: [featureTrain.shape[1]],
    })
  );
  model.add(tf.layers.dense({ units: numClasses, activation:
  "softmax" }));
  model.summary();

  const optimizer = tf.train.adam(params.learningRate);
  model.compile({
    optimizer: optimizer,
    loss: "categoricalCrossentropy",
    metrics: ["accuracy"],
  });
```

```
// Train the model with our features and labels
await model.fit(featureTrain, labelTrain, {
  epochs: params.epochs,
  validationData: [featureTest, labelTest],
});
// Save the model in our file system.
await model.save("file://model");
return model;
};
```

At the end of our format function, call this createModel function using createModel(trainingFeatures, trainingLabels, testingFeatures, testingLabels).

Now, if everything works fine and you run node train.js in your terminal, you should see the model training and find a model folder in your application!

In case something is not working as expected, here's what the complete train.js file should look like.

Listing 5-79. Complete code sample in train.js

```
const lineReader = require("line-reader");
var fs = require("fs");
const tf = require("@tensorflow/tfjs-node");

let justFeatures = [];
let justLabels = [];
const gestureClasses = ["letterA", "letterB", "letterC"];
let numClasses = gestureClasses.length;

let numSamplesPerGesture = 5;
let totalNumDataFiles = numSamplesPerGesture * numClasses;
let numPointsOfData = 6;
let numLinesPerFile = 100;
let totalNumDataPerFile = numPointsOfData * numLinesPerFile;
```

```
function readFile(file) {
  let allFileData = [];

  return new Promise((resolve, reject) => {
    fs.readFile(`data/${file}`, "utf8", (err, data) => {
      if (err) {
        reject(err);
      } else {
        lineReader.eachLine(`data/${file}`, function (line) {
          let dataArray = line
            .split(" ")
            .map((arrayItem) => parseFloat(arrayItem));
          allFileData.push(...dataArray);
          let concatArray = [...allFileData];

          if (concatArray.length === totalNumDataPerFile) {
            let label = file.split("_")[1];
            let labelIndex = gestureClasses.indexOf(label);
            resolve({ features: concatArray, label:
            labelIndex });
          }
        });
      }
    });
  });
}

const readDir = () =>
  new Promise((resolve, reject) =>
    fs.readdir(`data/`, "utf8", (err, data) =>
      err ? reject(err) : resolve(data)
    )
  );
```

```
(async () => {
  const filenames = await readDir();
  let allData = [];
  filenames.map(async (file) => {
    let originalContent = await readFile(file);
    allData.push(originalContent);
    if (allData.length === totalNumDataFiles) {
      format(allData);
    }
  });
})();

const format = (allData) => {
  let sortedData = allData.sort((a, b) => (a.label > b.label ?
  1 : -1));
  sortedData.map((item) => {
    createMultidimentionalArrays(justLabels, item.label, item.
    label);
    createMultidimentionalArrays(justFeatures, item.label,
    item.features);
  });

  const [trainingFeatures, trainingLabels, testingFeatures,
  testingLabels] = transformToTensor(justFeatures, justLabels);

  createModel(trainingFeatures, trainingLabels,
  testingFeatures, testingLabels);
};

function createMultidimentionalArrays(dataArray, index, item) {
  !dataArray[index] && dataArray.push([]);
  dataArray[index].push(item);
}
```

```
const transformToTensor = (features, labels) => {
  return tf.tidy(() => {
    const featureTrainings = [];
    const labelTrainings = [];
    const featureTests = [];
    const labelTests = [];
    for (let i = 0; i < gestureClasses.length; ++i) {
      const [featureTrain, labelTrain, featureTest, labelTest]
      = convertToTensors(features[i], labels[i], 0.2);
      featureTrainings.push(featureTrain);
      labelTrainings.push(labelTrain);
      featureTests.push(featureTest);
      labelTests.push(labelTest);
    }

    const concatAxis = 0;
    return [
      tf.concat(featureTrainings, concatAxis),
      tf.concat(labelTrainings, concatAxis),
      tf.concat(featureTests, concatAxis),
      tf.concat(labelTests, concatAxis),
    ];
  });
};

const convertToTensors = (featuresData, labelData, testSplit)
=> {
  if (featuresData.length !== labelData.length) {
    throw new Error(
      "features set and labels set have different numbers of
      examples"
    );
  }
```

```
  const [shuffledFeatures, shuffledLabels] = shuffleData(
    featuresData, labelData);

  const featuresTensor = tf.tensor2d(shuffledFeatures, [
    numSamplesPerGesture,
    totalNumDataPerFile,
  ]);
  const labelsTensor = tf.oneHot(
    tf.tensor1d(shuffledLabels).toInt(),
    numClasses
  );

  return split(featuresTensor, labelsTensor, testSplit);
};

const shuffleData = (features, labels) => {
  const indices = [...Array(numSamplesPerGesture).keys()];
  tf.util.shuffle(indices);

  const shuffledFeatures = [];
  const shuffledLabels = [];

  features.map((featuresArray, index) => {
    shuffledFeatures.push(features[indices[index]]);
    shuffledLabels.push(labels[indices[index]]);
  });

  return [shuffledFeatures, shuffledLabels];
};

const split = (featuresTensor, labelsTensor, testSplit) => {
  const numTestExamples = Math.round(numSamplesPerGesture *
  testSplit);
  const numTrainExamples = numSamplesPerGesture -
  numTestExamples;
```

```
  const trainingFeatures = featuresTensor.slice(
    [0, 0],
    [numTrainExamples, totalNumDataPerFile]
  );
  const testingFeatures = featuresTensor.slice(
    [numTrainExamples, 0],
    [numTestExamples, totalNumDataPerFile]
  );
  const trainingLabels = labelsTensor.slice(
    [0, 0],
    [numTrainExamples, numClasses]
  );
  const testingLabels = labelsTensor.slice(
    [numTrainExamples, 0],
    [numTestExamples, numClasses]
  );

  return [trainingFeatures, trainingLabels, testingFeatures,
testingLabels];
};

const createModel = async (xTrain, yTrain, xTest, yTest) => {
  const params = { learningRate: 0.1, epochs: 40 };
  const model = tf.sequential();
  model.add(
    tf.layers.dense({
      units: 10,
      activation: "sigmoid",
      inputShape: [xTrain.shape[1]],
    })
  );
```

```
model.add(tf.layers.dense({ units: numClasses, activation:
"softmax" }));
model.summary();

const optimizer = tf.train.adam(params.learningRate);
model.compile({
  optimizer: optimizer,
  loss: "categoricalCrossentropy",
  metrics: ["accuracy"],
});

await model.fit(xTrain, yTrain, {
  epochs: params.epochs,
  validationData: [xTest, yTest],
});

await model.save("file://model");
return model;
};
```

The training steps you should see in your terminal should look like the following figure.

```
Epoch 34 / 40
eta=0.0 ============================================================>
8ms 679us/step - acc=0.917 loss=0.214 val_acc=0.667 val_loss=1.45
Epoch 35 / 40
eta=0.0 ============================================================>
8ms 678us/step - acc=0.917 loss=0.214 val_acc=0.667 val_loss=1.45
Epoch 36 / 40
eta=0.0 ============================================================>
8ms 655us/step - acc=0.917 loss=0.212 val_acc=0.667 val_loss=1.46
Epoch 37 / 40
eta=0.0 ============================================================>
8ms 661us/step - acc=0.917 loss=0.211 val_acc=0.667 val_loss=1.47
Epoch 38 / 40
eta=0.0 ============================================================>
11ms 926us/step - acc=0.917 loss=0.210 val_acc=0.667 val_loss=1.48
Epoch 39 / 40
eta=0.0 ============================================================>
10ms 844us/step - acc=0.917 loss=0.209 val_acc=0.667 val_loss=1.49
Epoch 40 / 40
eta=0.0 ============================================================>
8ms 708us/step - acc=0.917 loss=0.208 val_acc=0.667 val_loss=1.51
```

Figure 5-56. *Sample output of the training steps*

The output of the model shows us that the last step of the training showed an accuracy of 0.9, which is really good!

Now, to test this with live data, let's move on to the last step of this project, using our model to generate predictions.

5.3.6 Live predictions

For this last step, let's create a new JavaScript file called predict.js.

We are going to create a new endpoint called '/predict', serve our index.html file, use similar web sockets code to send motion data from our phone to our server, and run live predictions.

A first small modification is in our initial index.js file in our front-end code. Instead of sending the motion data as a string, we need to replace it with the following data.

Listing 5-80. In index.js. Update the shape of the motion data sent via web sockets

```
let data = {
    xAcc: accelerometerData.x,
    yAcc: accelerometerData.y,
    zAcc: accelerometerData.z,
    xGyro: gyroscopeData.x,
    yGyro: gyroscopeData.y,
    zGyro: gyroscopeData.z,
};
socket.emit("motion data", data);
```

As the live data is going to have to be fed to the model, it is easier to send an object of numbers rather than go through the same formatting we went during the training process.

Then, our `predict.js` file is going to look very similar to our `server.js` file at the exception of an additional `predict` function that feeds live data to the model and generate a prediction about the gesture.

Listing 5-81. In predict.js. Complete code for the predict.js file

```
const tf = require("@tensorflow/tfjs-node");
const express = require("express");
const app = express();
var http = require("http").createServer(app);
const io = require("socket.io")(http);

let liveData = [];
let predictionDone = false;
let model;
const gestureClasses = ["letterA", "letterB", "letterC"];
```

```
// Create new endpoint
app.use("/predict", express.static(__dirname + "/"));

io.on("connection", async function (socket) {
  // Load the model
  model = await tf.loadLayersModel("file://model/model.json");
  socket.on("motion data", function (data) {
    predictionDone = false;
    // This makes sure the data has the same shape as the one
    used during training. 600 represents 6 values (x,y,z for
    accelerometer and gyroscope), collected 100 times.
    if (liveData.length < 600) {
      liveData.push(
        data.xAcc,
        data.yAcc,
        data.zAcc,
        data.xGyro,
        data.yGyro,
        data.zGyro
      );
    }
  });

  socket.on("end motion data", function () {
    if (!predictionDone && liveData.length) {
      predictionDone = true;
      predict(model, liveData);
      liveData = [];
    }
  });
});
```

```
const predict = (model, newSampleData) => {
  tf.tidy(() => {
    const inputData = newSampleData;
    // Create a tensor from live data
    const input = tf.tensor2d([inputData], [1, 600]);
    const predictOut = model.predict(input);
    // Access the highest probability
    const winner = gestureClasses[predictOut.argMax(-1).
    dataSync()[0]];
    console.log(winner);
  });
};
```

```
http.listen(process.env.PORT || 3000);
```

If you run the preceding code sample using node predict.js, visit the page on '/predict' on your phone, and execute one of the three gestures we trained. While holding the screen down, you should see a prediction in the terminal once you release the screen!

When running live predictions, you might come across the following error. This happens when a gesture is executed too fast and the amount of data collected was lower than our 600 value, meaning the data does not have the correct shape for the model to use it. If you try again a bit slower, it should be working.

```
Error: Based on the provided shape, [1,600], the tensor should have 600 values but has
  408
```

Figure 5-57. *Possible error when a gesture is executed too fast*

Now that our live predictions work, you could move on to changing some parameters used to create the model to see how it impacts the predictions, or train different gestures, or even send the prediction back to the front end using web sockets to create an interactive application. The main goal of this last section was to cover the steps involved into creating your own machine learning model.

Over the last few pages we learned to access hardware data using the Generic Sensor API, set up a server and web sockets to communicate and share data, save motion data into files, process and transform it, as well as create, train, and use a model to predict live gestures!

Hopefully it gives you a better idea of all the possibilities offered by machine learning and TensorFlow.js.

However, it was a lot of new information if you are new to it, especially this last section was quite advanced and experimental, so I would not expect you to understand everything and feel completely comfortable yet.

Feel free to go back over the code samples, take your time, and play around with building small prototypes if you are interested.

CHAPTER 6

Machine learning in production

Now that you hopefully feel more comfortable experimenting with machine learning and building applications using different models and inputs, let's talk about the different aspects of putting machine learning models and systems into production.

Before we start, it is important to know that this chapter is not going to be a deep dive into how to set up a machine learning pipeline yourself using Kubernetes clusters, configuring load balancers, and so on, as this is in general a task taken on by a DevOps or infrastructure teams. However, it is important to understand the challenges that come with productionizing machine learning models, so we are instead going to explain some of them, as well as introduce a few different tools that should help you add machine learning in your production applications if you do not have the opportunity to work with a dedicated team.

6.1 Challenges

Putting machine learning in production creates a different set of challenges than the ones we might have had so far.

In the personal projects we have built in this book, we were the only user and we were running everything locally. We were more in a proof-of-concept phase. In production, not only an application will be used

© Charlie Gerard 2021
C. Gerard, *Practical Machine Learning in JavaScript*,
https://doi.org/10.1007/978-1-4842-6418-8_6

by hundreds, thousands, or even millions of users, it will also be built by multiple teams. As a result, your system will have to be able to adapt and handle more challenges.

6.1.1 Scalability

The purpose of putting machine learning models in production is to make it part of the application your users are interacting with every day. As a result, it should be able to handle a potential large amount of requests.

Either it be for a startup or a large corporation, running machine learning models requires a lot of CPUs, GPUs, and RAM, meaning you will have to make sure your system can support running the model for all users.

6.1.2 High availability

Most web applications you have worked on and will work on are expected to be available 24/7 to serve user requests.

If you decide to add machine learning models to these systems, they will also need to have a high availability.

No matter if you decide to update a model, scale it to a wider audience, or test new tools, it is very important to make sure the model is still running properly as you experiment.

6.1.3 Observability

The systems we work on are very volatile. Things can change very fast in many ways. Your user interface changes as you release new features, spikes of users can happen in different geographical locations, third-party providers can fail, and so on.

Such volatility means that models and their predictions should be watched closely. Not only is it about verifying that the model is not failing to generate predictions, it is also about regularly checking if the inputs and outputs are correct.

6.1.4 Reusability

Depending on the models you have built and are running in your application, it is sometimes important to think about their reusability.

For example, the company booking.com runs multiple models in production including one to determine if a hotel is family-friendly.

Based on different criteria, a model can highlight family-friendly hotels in both the details page of a hotel or as a filter in the results page. Similarly to how different UI components can be reusable across a front-end application, building your models so they can be reused on different pages can ensure that you are making the most of them.

Creating and testing a machine learning model being a time-consuming task, model reutilization makes this investment more productive.

Moreover, reusability ensures that models can be shared between different teams facing similar problems and can avoid wasting time re-creating models from scratch.

Now that we've briefly covered a few of the challenges presented by productionizing machine learning models, let's look into the life cycle of a ML project.

6.2 Machine learning life cycle

The following diagram is a visual guide for the concept of Continuous Delivery for Machine Learning (CD4ML) popularized by Martin Fowler.

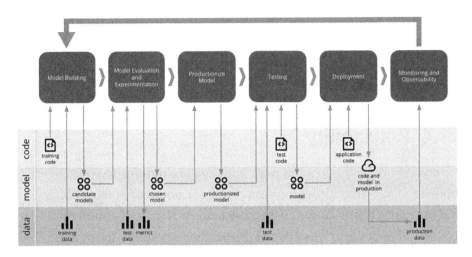

Figure 6-1. *Phases of Continuous Delivery for Machine Learning. Source:* `https://martinfowler.com/articles/cd4ml.html`

In this diagram, we can see outlined six different phases:

Model building is about understanding the problem, preparing the data, extracting features, and writing the initial code to create the model.

Model evaluation and experimentation is about selecting features, hyperparameter tuning, comparing algorithms, and overall experimenting with different solutions.

Productionizing the model is the step that goes from experimentation or research to preparing it for deployment.

Testing focuses on ensuring that the model and the code we are about to deploy to production behave as we expect, and that the results match the ones observed during the second phase of evaluation and experimentation.

Deployment is getting the model into production.

Finally, m**onitoring and observability** is about ensuring that the model behaves as expected in the production environment.

One of the main differences between a standard software project life cycle and a machine learning project is in the way these phases should repeat.

As the arrow suggests from the last phase (Monitoring and Observability) back to the first one (Model Building), we should make decisions about our models based on information collected after seeing how it behaves in production.

Models should be updated or abandoned based on this information.

Based on your application, your model needs to be regularly retrained with new data to avoid becoming obsolete.

For example, a platform like AutoScout24 that helps users sell their vehicles online uses machine learning to predict the price range at which people should sell their car, based on a few parameters including the brand, the year of production, and the model.

If they do not retrain their model regularly with real user data, their prediction will quickly be out of date and not represent the real value of their users' vehicle on the market. As a result, people could either undersell or struggle to sell their car because the prices are not adjusted to the current market.

This cycle that retrains the model with new data can be done manually or automatically.

Also, not all of these phases have to be executed by the same engineers.

The first two phases of model building and experimentation can and/or should be done by data scientists or machine learning engineers. The following phases should be undertaken by DevOps engineers or software engineers with experience in deploying applications to production, like the following image illustrates.

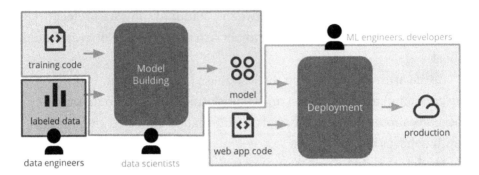

Figure 6-2. *Types of engineers per phase.*

Seeing how different parts of this life cycle are separated by types of engineer leads us to talk about machine learning systems

6.3 Machine learning systems

In this book, we have talked a lot about how to use pre-trained models and generate predictions; however, machine learning systems are made up of a lot more components.

For example, if you cannot find a pre-trained models for your application and decide to create your own, you will also need to think about data collection, verification, feature extraction, and monitoring, as the following figure shows.

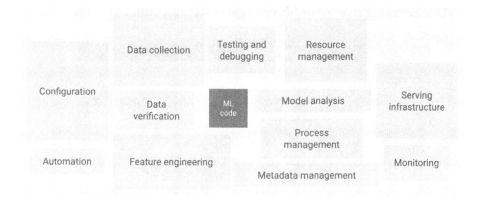

Figure 6-3. *Components of a machine learning system. Source:*
`https://cloud.google.com/solutions/machine-learning/mlops-`
`continuous-delivery-and-automation-pipelines-in-machine-`
`learning`

Using a machine learning model in production requires you to set up a
certain pipeline.

Not only your model needs to be served, but you will need to think
about how to collect new data and retrain your model so it does not
become obsolete, how and what to monitor, and so on.

Luckily, you do not need to build all of these components yourself.
Platforms like TensorFlow Extended (TFX) offer an end-to-end solution for
deploying production ML pipelines.

TFX includes different components that can help you set up a machine
learning pipeline like TensorFlow Data Validation to help you understand
your data, TensorFlow Transform to help you preprocess your data and
convert it between formats as needed, and TensorFlow Serving to support
model versioning and ensuring high performance with concurrent models.

The benefit of using such platforms is that most of your ML pipeline
can be set up in a single platform, reducing complexity in the setup and
maintenance, as well as being able to leverage the work of dedicated teams
at Google, to give you more confidence in the performance and reliability
of your system.

The following is an example of a typical TFX pipeline.

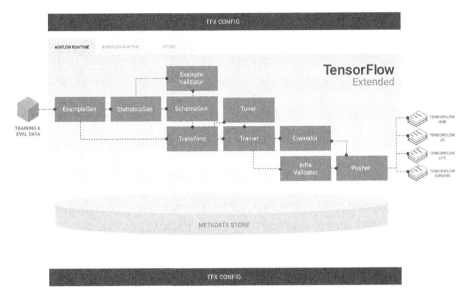

Figure 6-4. *Standard TFX pipeline*

To get a better understanding of what TFX can do, let's go through each of these components:

- First, **ExampleGen** is the initial input component that consumes external files and ingests the data into the pipeline.

- **StatisticsGen** is in charge of calculating statistics for the dataset that will be used to generate a schema.

- **SchemaGen** generates the schema that contains information about your input data, for example, data types for each feature or if the feature has to be present every time. An example of what a schema could look like is shown in the following image.

```
...
feature {
  name: "age"
  value_count {
    min: 1
    max: 1
  }
  type: FLOAT
  presence {
    min_fraction: 1
    min_count: 1
  }
}
feature {
  name: "capital-gain"
  value_count {
    min: 1
    max: 1
  }
  type: FLOAT
  presence {
    min_fraction: 1
    min_count: 1
  }
}
...
```

Figure 6-5. *Example schema. Source:* `www.tensorflow.org/tfx/ guide/schemagen`

- **ExampleValidator** is used to identify anomalies in the training data.

- **Transform** will actually use the schema generated from the SchemaGen component and perform feature engineering on the data emitted from ExampleGen to generate a SavedModel instance that will be used by the following component.

- **Trainer** uses the Python TensorFlow API to train models.

- **Tuner** does hyperparameter tuning, meaning it chooses a set of optimal parameters to use with a model.

- **Evaluator** performs analysis on the results of your model to ensure that it is good to be pushed to production.

- **InfraValidator** is responsible for validating the model in the model serving infrastructure. It launches a sandboxed model server with the model and checks if it can be loaded and queried.

- **Pusher** is the component pushing a validated model to a deployment target.

If this seems a bit complicated, it is totally normal. As I mentioned at the beginning of this chapter, I would not expect any person reading this book to understand straight away all the components needed in a machine learning pipeline.

As it is unlikely that you will have to set one up yourself, this information is mainly presented so you get an idea of the components involved in setting up a system when working with deploying a custom model.

Now that we briefly went over what a standard TFX pipeline looks like, let's go back and talk about pipelines more broadly. What are the necessities of building a pipeline?

If we look back at the image at the beginning of this section, the machine learning code to create the model actually represents a very small portion of the system.

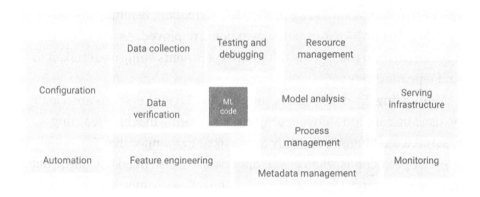

Figure 6-6. *Components of a machine learning system. Source:* `https://cloud.google.com/solutions/machine-learning/mlops-continuous-delivery-and-automation-pipelines-in-machine-learning`

The rest is composed of elements such as data collection, automation, testing, analysis, and so on, where you need to apply DevOps principles to ML systems.

This kind of system works similarly to a software system in the sense that you need it to be reliable and have short development cycles but differs in the following ways:

Diversity of skills: If you work on a production application that uses machine learning models, your team will likely involve data scientists that will need to interact with the system but may not have experience or knowledge of software practices. Your system will have to take this into account by having components ML researchers can use.

Model serving: There seems to be three different ways to serve models in production. It can either be done with an **embedded model** where you treat it as a dependency packaged with the application, a **model as a service (MAAS)** where the model is wrapped in a separate service that can be deployed and updated independently, and a **model as data** where the model is also independent but ingested as data at runtime.

Experiment tracking: Machine learning models go through a lot of experimentation before being pushed to production, resulting in a lot of the code being thrown away and never being deployed. As a result, it is important to keep track of the different experiments being undertaken to avoid repeating them.

Monitoring: Even though monitoring and logging systems are usually also used in standard software projects, monitoring machine learning models is a bit different. Not only do we need to monitor that the model generates predictions when given input data, we also need to capture data about how our model is behaving using the following metrics – **model inputs** (track what data is being fed to the model), **interpretability of outputs** (understanding how models are making predictions), model outputs themselves, and **model fairness** (analysis outputs for bias).

Testing: Different types of tests can be introduced in a machine learning workflow. We can test the model quality by looking at error rates and accuracy, the validity of the data by comparing it to schemas generated, or even attempt to test model bias and fairness. The following is an example of test pyramid for machine learning systems.

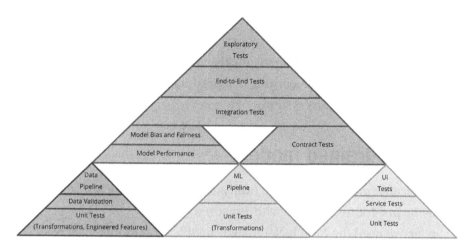

Figure 6-7. *Example of test pyramid. Source:* `https://martinfowler.com/articles/cd4ml.html`

Even though this kind of system might be the responsibility of an infrastructure team, as a developer, you should still be involved in setting up a way for the application to interact with the model.

As a result, you will have to ask yourself questions such as the following:

- How to write an API that will generate predictions from the model?

- How to best deploy that API to production?

- What kind of data needs to be collected?

- What information should the API return?

Now that we briefly covered the different components of a machine learning system, let's go through some of the tools currently available to make the use of machine learning in production easier.

6.4 Tools

In this last section, we are going to quickly cover some tools you can use if you want to add machine learning in a production application without having to set up a complex system.

6.4.1 Pre-trained models

Hopefully, after going through the projects in this book, you are familiar with using pre-trained models with TensorFlow.js.

So far, we used the MobileNet image classification model, PoseNet, the Toxicity Classifier, speech commands, Facemesh, Handpose, and the Question Answering model; however, there are a few more.

Indeed, if you decide to explore further, you will see that there also exist a face landmark detection model, an object detection model, a body segmentation model, and a few more.

However, pre-trained models do not have to be developed by the TensorFlow.js team to be usable with TensorFlow.js.

Keras models typically created using Python can be saved in different formats and converted to TensorFlow.js Layers format to be loaded with the framework.

As a result, if you find an open source model you are interested in working with, feel free to check if it can be converted to the format that works with TensorFlow.js so you can load it in a JavaScript application.

6.4.2 APIs

To make it easier for developers to implement machine learning in production applications, technology companies like Amazon, Google, and Microsoft have been working on developing ML services available as APIs.

For example, Amazon currently has multiple APIs for services including image and video analysis, personalized recommendations, real-time translation, advanced text analysis, chatbots, and fraud prevention.

For example, Amazon currently has APIs including

- Comprehend for advanced text analysis

- CodeGuru for automated code reviews

- Lex for chatbots

- Textract for document analysis

- Detector for fraud prevention

- Recognition for image and video analysis

- Polly for text to speech

Google Cloud offers APIs such as

- **Vision AI**: To get image insights, detect objects, faces, and text

- **Video intelligence API**: To recognize objects, places, and actions in stored and streaming video

- **Speech-to-text API**: To accurately convert speech into text

And Microsoft has a suite of tools called Cognitive Services with APIs including a content moderator service, a QnA Maker, a speaker recognition service that can identify and verify the people speaking based on audio, and similar APIs around image and text recognition.

6.4.3 Serving platforms

Finally, if you are more interested in building and serving a custom model, here are some tools that aim at making it simpler.

The Google Cloud AI platform as well as Amazon Web Services and Microsoft offer more complete solutions for you to serve your custom machine learning projects; however, other model serving platforms can be found such as the open source BentoML, Seldon, or kaos by KI labs.

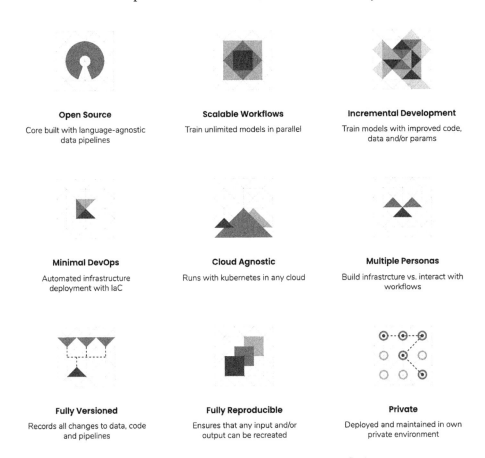

Open Source
Core built with language-agnostic data pipelines

Scalable Workflows
Train unlimited models in parallel

Incremental Development
Train models with improved code, data and/or params

Minimal DevOps
Automated infrastructure deployment with IaC

Cloud Agnostic
Runs with kubernetes in any cloud

Multiple Personas
Build infrastrcture vs. interact with workflows

Fully Versioned
Records all changes to data, code and pipelines

Fully Reproducible
Ensures that any input and/or output can be recreated

Private
Deployed and maintained in own private environment

Figure 6-8. *Features of kaos. Source:* `https://ki-labs.com/kaos/#features`

Even though teams may be tempted to rely on tools from Google, Microsoft, or Amazon, these platforms do not often give you the freedom you may want in picking your tooling. They optimize for the use of their own offerings and sometimes make it complicated to integrate with other third-party tools.

Besides, depending on the size of your application, using these platforms may be overengineering.

Overall, there are multiple options available when it comes to productionizing machine learning models. However, as this is still something most companies are not doing, the standards are not set and will probably evolve. As a result, if this is an area you are interested in learning more about, you should definitely do some extra research and experimentation.

CHAPTER 7

Bias in machine learning

In my opinion, this book would not be complete without mentioning the topic of bias in machine learning.

As we give the ability to computers to generate predictions and rely on them in production applications that people will interact with, it is essential to spend some time thinking about the consequences and impact of using this technology.

In this last chapter, we are going to talk about the different types of biases, why this is an issue and what can be done to minimize it in our machine learning systems.

7.1 What is bias?

If we refer to the definition from the Oxford dictionary, bias is

> *a strong feeling in favour of or against one group of people, or one side in an argument, often not based on fair judgement.*

—Quote source:
www.oxfordlearnersdictionaries.com/definition/
english/bias_1?q=bias

© Charlie Gerard 2021
C. Gerard, *Practical Machine Learning in JavaScript*,
https://doi.org/10.1007/978-1-4842-6418-8_7

When it comes to data science, there can be different types of biases, including

- **Confirmation bias**: This can happen when the person performing the data analysis wants to prove a predetermined assumption and will intentionally exclude particular variables from an analysis until it comes to the wanted conclusion.

- **Selection bias or sample bias**: This happens when the sample of data used is not a good reflection of the population.

- **Prejudice bias**: Result of training data that is influenced by cultural or other stereotypes. For example, if we train an algorithm to recognize people at work based on images found online, a lot of them show men coding, for example, and women in the kitchen. As a result, the model will be predicting men as being more likely coders and women cook, which is incorrect and replicating biases found online.

If you are not familiar with the topic of bias in machine learning, you might be wondering why it is a problem.

Humans are biased in many ways; we can make unfounded assumptions about people or situations that can lead to discrimination. However, when this bias makes it into products or systems used in our daily lives and developed to make decisions for us and about us, this can have terrible widespread consequences that should not be ignored.

Let's look at some examples.

7.2 Examples of bias in machine learning

Over the next couple of pages, we are going to look at two examples of situations where biased machine learning models were used in real applications.

7.2.1 Gender bias

A few years ago, Google Translate made the news with translations that were revealing the algorithms' gender bias. When translating some words from the Turkish language to English, the one pronoun "o", which covers every kind of singular third person in Turkish, was translated to a gendered pronoun in English, resulting in the following biased results.

Figure 7-1. *Google Translate showing biased results*

As you can see in the preceding image, even though the Turkish language did not specify a certain gender for each term, Google Translate guessed a particular one, resulting in stereotypes such as matching the word "doctor" with the pronoun "he" and the word "nurse" with "she".

Google has now updated their algorithm to try to prevent such biases from happening by now displaying both feminine and masculine translations for a single word.

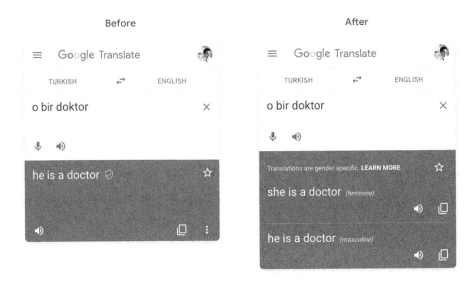

Figure 7-2. *Google Translate showing results with multiple pronouns*

Even though this is an improvement, the fault was not necessarily on the algorithm itself but most likely due to the fact that the data used to train it probably contained biased information.

Besides, displaying both "she" and "he" pronouns does not take into account people who use the pronoun "they", which should be included to achieve better fairness.

7.2.2 Racial bias

One of the most impactful examples of biased machine learning algorithm used in the past few years is with a software powered by AI called COMPAS.

This software has been used by judges in courtrooms to generate risk assessments and forecast which criminals are most likely to reoffend based on responses to 137 survey questions.

The issue with using this algorithm is that it was discovered that, when it was wrong about its predictions, the results were displaying differently for black and white offenders.

Black offenders were labelled as higher risk even though their chance of reoffending was lower, whereas white offenders were labelled as lower risk even though they had a higher probability to reoffend.

Figure 7-3. *COMPAS software results*

The fact that such erroneous predictions were used in the justice system is already a serious issue, but the scale at which it was used makes this even more concerning.

Considering the United States imprisons a large number of people each year, one can only imagine the amount of incorrect convictions.

Besides, as the company behind COMPAS, called Northpointe, refused to disclose the details of their algorithm, it made it impossible for researchers to evaluate the extent of its unfairness.

These are only two examples of situations where bias can be introduced in machine learning algorithms. There are unfortunately plenty more and I would recommend to dive deeper into the topic.

7.3 Potential solutions

Even though bias in machine learning cannot be completely eradicated, there are a few options to minimize it.

7.3.1 Framing the problem

Before working on building a model and generating predictions, data scientists need to decide what problem they are trying to solve. It is already at this stage that some bias can be found. If you are building a model for a credit company that wants to automatically evaluate the "creditworthiness" of people, there are already decisions made around the concept what defines someone who is worthy of getting a credit that might embed some unfairness and discrimination.

For example, a company can decide that it wants to maximize its profit margins, meaning creditworthiness will be based on how rich a client is as they will probably contract bigger loans. Otherwise, it can also decide that it would rather focus on maximizing the amount of loans contracted, no matter if clients can afford them or not.

Overall the issue lies within the fact that these decisions are made with business objectives in mind, and not fairness, even though they will end up impacting real people in many ways.

If an algorithm predicted that the giving subprime loans was an effective way to maximize profit, the company would end up engaging in predatory behavior even if it wasn't the direct intention.

7.3.2 Collecting the data

This may be a more frequent example of how bias makes its way into machine learning models and can show up in two ways.

Incorrect representation of reality

You may have heard of cases where collecting data that was unrepresentative of reality caused a machine learning model to generate incorrect predictions.

For example, in face recognition, if an algorithm is trained with more images representing people with light-skinned faces than dark-skinned faces, the model created will inevitably be better at recognizing light-skinned faces.

To try to prevent this kind of discrimination, analyzing the data you are using before feeding it to an algorithm will give you an idea of its quality and its potential in generating more fair predictions.

In general, if you decide to use a pre-trained model, there should be a link documented for you to have a look at the dataset used. If you cannot find it, I would request it to the company or person sharing the model.

If you are unable to verify the quality of the data, I would advise to find a different model.

If you found the original dataset and noticed that it was lacking diversity and was not a good representation of reality, you could either decide not to use the model trained using this data, or you could decide to leverage it, collect some additional, more diverse data, and apply transfer learning to generate a new, less biased model to use in your application.

If you take the route of collecting your own data and not rely on some existing model, I would advise to start by analyzing what diversity means in your particular case, what problem is your model going to solve, who will it be used on, what sources are you planning on using to collect the data, are these sources representative of reality, and so on.

The analysis work is essential to raise potential issues or concerns early and build a model that will minimize the perpetuation of biases.

Reflection of existing prejudices

A second issue when it comes to collecting data is in using some that contains existing prejudices.

Some companies use some of their internal historical data to train machine learning models to automate tasks.

For example, a couple of years ago in 2018, Amazon realized that their internal AI recruiting tool was biased against women.

They had been using data gathered for the past 10 years of job applications to rate new candidates from 0 to 5 stars. However, as most people hired to work at Amazon were males, the model had deduced that male candidates were preferable.

Looking at historical hiring data and analyzing thousands of resumes, the model's logic was that Amazon did not like resumes with the word "women" in it.

As a result, any resume that was containing this word, for example, "Captain of the women's team" or "Studied at a women's college," was getting a lower rating than the ones not mentioning it.

Even though this made the news in 2018, Amazon had realized its new system was not rating candidates in a gender-neutral way, since 2015.

A way to prevent this type of discrimination is related to the section earlier, analyzing the data you are using. The fact that data is internal does not mean it is unbiased. However, considering that this data had been collected over the past 10 years, we can agree that it might be too much data to analyze manually. I would still advise to collect a random set of samples and have people assess their fairness and diversity.

Besides, when using a model for a task as important as hiring, I would hope that some testing of the model was done before using it. Bias in hiring is a well-known issue and can take many forms. As a result, if you decide to build or use a recruitment software that relies on machine learning, I would advise to test it for different biases, from gender to educational background, to ethnicity, and so on.

7.3.3 Data preparation

Another place where bias can be introduced is when preparing the data. Even if you have analyzed your data and made sure that it is diverse and represents the reality of the environment it is going to be used for, the preparation stage also needs some attention.

This phase involves selecting attributes you want your algorithm to consider when learning and generating predictions and can be described as more of an art than a science.

Often, some experimentations with attributes and parameters are needed to fine-tune a model.

However, you also need to make sure that reaching high accuracy does not also introduce bias. While the impact of experimenting with attributes on accuracy is measurable, its impact on bias isn't.

In the case of the recruitment tool at Amazon, attributes could have been candidates' gender, education level, years of experience, programming languages, geographical location, and so on.

For the purpose of hiring someone as an engineer, for example, a person's gender should not matter at all so should be omitted as an attribute to train the model.

A person's geographical location would only matter if the company cannot sponsor visas to relocate.

As a result, to maximize fairness, a model trained to rank candidates should take into consideration attributes impacting their skill level, including years of experience and programming languages.

It could also use education level, but this could introduce some bias toward people who have had the privilege of getting higher education.

In the technology industry, many very good developers have not taken the path of getting a computer science degree, so using this as an attribute could result in ranking people lower even though, in practice, they possess the right skills and would be great employees.

Hopefully this example demonstrates how important the data preparation phase is, no matter if you have already spent some time making sure the dataset you are using is diverse.

7.3.4 Team diversity

Finally, minimizing bias in machine learning also lies in the makeup of the teams working on developing models.

We all have biases, and an efficient way to mitigate diversity deficits is in improving diversity in your teams.

You can imagine that issues found in facial recognition models would have been prevented if the teams working on them included more non-white people.

Not only would this help in testing the predictions of a model to make sure their accuracy is high across a diverse set of faces, it would also improve the overall process.

Previous phases of framing the problem, collecting, and preparing the data would benefit from people with different backgrounds, life experiences, and so on. Potential issues could be raised early and influence the development of a more fair model while still working toward high accuracy.

Not only is this an ethical challenge but also a technical one. How good really is a facial recognition model if it's mostly accurate when used on light-skinned people? If the goal of machine learning is to develop models with the highest accuracy, then the real technical challenge is in high accuracy across a diverse set of samples.

7.4 Challenges

Unfortunately, even though the previous section stated a few of the potential solutions to reduce bias in machine learning, this issue is a difficult one to fix and will probably still be present for a while.

In this section, we are going to go through a few challenges of mitigating bias.

Unknowns

It can be unclear where bias was introduced in a system. Even if you work with a diverse dataset, make sure to use attributes that do not alter the fairness of the predictions; it is sometimes difficult to understand how a model generated a certain result.

In the case of Amazon and its gender-biased recruiting tool, once they realized that the model was picking up words like "women's" to rank candidates lower, they updated their model to ignore explicitly gendered words; however, that was not enough. They later discovered that the updated system was still picking up on implicitly gendered words that were more commonly found on men's resumes, such as "executed" and "captured", and was using this to made decisions.

Fairness is relative

Another challenge when it comes to bias in machine learning is around the fact that not everyone agrees on what is considered fair or unfair. Unfortunately, more work has been done on the technical side than on the ethics side of AI, so there are no real standards, regulations, and policies at this point when it comes to designing ethical AI applications.

Some companies like Google are sharing their principles when it comes to developing AI solutions that other companies can also decide to adopt; however, these should not be considered regulations. For example, so far, Google's AI principles include the following objectives for AI applications:

- Be socially beneficial

- Avoid creating or reinforcing unfair bias

- Be built and tested for safety

- Be accountable to people

- Incorporate privacy design principles

- Uphold high standards of scientific excellence

- Be made available for uses that accord with these principles

Even though these are a good start, we should hope that governments will soon provide real regulations around the development and use of machine learning models and how to assess their fairness, so we can hope to avoid the widespread implementation of biased systems.

In this chapter, we covered briefly some examples of situations where biased machine learning models were used and the consequences, as well as some possible solutions.

If you are interested in learning more about this topic, I would highly recommend you read the books *Weapons of Math Destruction* by Cathy O'Neil and *Algorithms of Oppression* by Safiya Noble, in which the authors cover this fascinating subject in much more depth.

Index

A

Abstractive text summarization, 102

Application programming
interfaces (APIs), 300–301

Artificial intelligence, 2

Attention deficit hyperactivity
disorder (ADHD), 95

Audio data
accessing data, 138–143
acoustic activity
recognition, 136
biodiversity research/
protection, 171–172
health, 169
limitations
data quality, 174–175
interactions, 177
single activity, 176–177
user experience, 177–182
meaning, 135–136
microphones, 138
personal devices, 136
predictions
callback function, 160
file structure, 158
loading, 158
metadata files, 158
setupModel function,
159–160, 162–163
source code, 162
speech commands
model, 157
transfer learning API, 164
recording samples
HTML file, 165–166
listen method, 167
source code, 168
train method, 166
web interface, 165
sound, 137–138
Teachable Machine interface
background noise
section, 153
browser window, 154
custom section, 154
experiments, 152
open source GitHub, 156
predictions, 155
visualizations
frequency charts, 144
spectrogram, 144, 147–154
waveform, 143
web accessibility, 173–174
Automation tools, 98–99

B

Biases
  AI objectives, 315
  COMPAS software results, 309
  confirmation, 306
  data preparation, 313–314
  Google translate, 307–308
  meaning, 305
  mitigating bias, 315–317
  potential solution, 310
    creditworthiness, 310
    existing prejudices, 312
    incorrect representation, 311
    team developing
      models, 314
  prejudice bias, 306
  racial bias, 308–310
  selection/sample bias, 306
Bidirectional Encoder
      Representations from
      Transformers (BERT)
      model, 102
Body/movement tracking, 182
  facemesh
    full JavaScript code, 191–193
    loading file, 185–187
    predictions, 191–194
    project code, 194–200
    visualization, 183–185
  Handpose model
    importing, 200–202
    JavaScript code, 205–207
    key points, 199

paper gesture, 211
predictions, 203–206
project screenshot, 208–220
scissors, 209, 214
PoseNet
  drawSkeleton
    functions, 236
  HTML code, 231–235
  importing and loading,
    222–223
  meaning, 219
  poseDetectionFrame
    function, 238
  predictions, 223–231
  visualization, 220, 235–245

C

Cognitive behavioral therapy (CBT)
  companies, 91–95
  EndeavorRx, 95
  reSET, 92
  Woebot application, 91–92
  Wysa screenshot, 93–94
Convolutional neural
      networks (CNN), 18–20

D

Deep learning, 3

E, F

Extractive text summarization, 101

G

Google Cloud Provider (GCP)
platform, 103

H

Hardware data
browser output, 246
data processing
convertToTensors
function, 266–267
formatted data, 263
multidimensional
arrays, 265
output tensor, 269
readDir and readFile
function, 260–263
shuffleData function, 268
sorting/formatting
data, 264–265
train.js file, 270–273
gyroscope/accelerometer
data, 248–251
JavaScript code, 252
meaning, 245
model creation/training,
274–282
motion data, 252
predict.js file, 282–286
server.js file, 254
set up web sockets, 251–259
web sensors, 247–248

Healthcare, 18–20
Hyperparameter tuning, 37

I, J

Interactive education tool
code building, 108
dorothyVaughan.json file, 122
home page, 109
katherineJohnson.json file, 120
loading project, 111–113
maryJackson.json file, 121
prediction page, 116–125
public figure, 110
questions/display, 110
selection page, 113–115
Web Speech API
input data, 125
language recognition,
126–130
onresult method, 130–131
onspeechend code, 131–132
optional parameters, 126
QNA model, 132
SpeechRecognition
instance, 126
SpeechSynthesis
code, 133–134

K, L

K-nearest neighbors algorithm
(KNN), 16–17

M

Machine learning
  algorithms, 5
    ConvNet, 16–18
    K-nearest neighbors, 15–16
    Naive Bayes, 14
  Art modeling, 23–24
  artificial intelligence, 2
  biases, 305
  categories, 8
  CT scans, 3
  deep learning, 3
  healthcare, 18–20
  home automation, 20–21
  labeled data, 10
  meaning, 1
  models, 6–7
  neural network, 5–6
  reinforcement learning, 12–13
  representation, 1–2
  semi-supervised learning, 13
  social good, 21–23
  supervised learning, 9–10
  training process, 7
  unsupervised learning, 10–11

N, O

Naive Bayes algorithm, 14
Named entity recognition
  (NER), 100–101
Natural language processing, (NLP)
  bag-of-words, 68–71
  concepts, 68
  home automation, 20
  stop words, 73
  text lemmatization/stemming, 73
  tokenization, 71–72
  vocabulary/corpus, 69
Neural network, 5–6

P, Q

Prejudice bias, 306
Pre-trained models
  classification, 50
  classify() method, 36–37
  clearer background, 52
  companies/institutions, 35
  console output, 48
  dispose method, 53
  front-end framework, 47
  HTML file, 54
  hyper-parameter tuning, 37
  image capture, 50
  image classification
    project, 36, 45–46
  inputs properties, 48–49
  JavaScript code, 47, 55
  live object classification, 51
  loading function, 47
  meaning, 34
  mobilenet model, 35–46
  modules, 47
  prediction result, 51
  repository model, 53
  transfer learning (*see* Transfer
    learning)

script tags, 46

webcam object, 49–50

Production applications

APIs, 300–301

challenges, 287

high availability, 288

life cycle

building/experimentation, 291

continuous delivery, 289–290

deployment, 290

evaluation/experimentation, 290

model building, 290

monitoring/observability, 290

testing, 290

ML system

components, 293–297

experiment tracking, 298

model serving, 298

monitoring/logging systems, 298

results, 299

schema output, 295

standard TFX pipeline, 294

TensorFlow Extended (TFX), 293

testing, 298

observability, 288

pre-trained models, 300

reusability, 289

scalability, 288

serving platforms, 301–303

volatility, 289

Pseudo-labeling, 13

R

Rainforest connection project, 22

Reinforcement learning, 12–13

S

Selection/sample bias, 306

Semi-supervised learning, 13

Sentence tokenization, 71

Sentiment analysis

automation tools, 98–99

categories, 68

cognitive assistants/computer therapy, 91–95

meaning, 67

NLP (*see* Natural language processing, (NLP))

social media monitoring, 95–97

TensorFlow.js, 74

categories, 74

fixed-length vectors, 78

HTML tags, 80

importing model, 74

JavaScript code, 81–83

loadModel function, 75

metadata file, 76

predictions, 75–80

source code, 80–84

Sentiment analysis (*cont.*)
    text classification (*see* Text
        classification tools)
    toxicity (*see* Toxicity Classifier)
Social media monitoring
    tool, 95–97
Spammy phrase *vs.* Non-spammy
    phrase, 71
Spectrogram
    amplitude, 145
    frequency data, 149
    getAudioData function, 148–150
    HTML file, 148
    image data, 149
    JavaScript, 148
    meaning, 144
    output, 145
Supervised learning, 9–10

T

TensorFlow.js, 25
    accessing data, 30–31
    creation, 26–29
    creation/training model, 41
    features, 34
    flat arrays, 29
    iterations, 43
    memory, 33–34
    multidimensional tensors, 28
    operations, 31–33
    predictions, 43
    pre-trained model, 34–38
    sentiment analysis, 74–84

text classification tools, 102
tidy method, 33
transfer learning, 38–41
visual representation, 25
Text classification tools, 99
    intent analysis, 99
    named entity recognition,
        100–101
    TensorFlow.js
        browser's console, 106–108
        config object, 103
        custom configurations, 103
        findAnswers()
            method, 104
        HTML code, 105
        importing code, 102
        index.js file, 105
        interactive education
            tool, 108–134
        MobileBERT model, 102
        predictions, 104
    text summarization, 101–102
Text lemmatization/stemming, 73
Toxicity Classifier
    different labels, 84
    HTML file/script tags, 85
    import, 85
    predictions
        array, 86
        classify() method, 86
        detailed view, 87
        identity_attack label, 89
        match value, 88
        potential issue, 90

probabilities array, 88

return values, 89

Transfer learning, 38–41

  addExample function, 59–60

  buttons elements, 60

  conv_preds, 59

  HTML code, 63–65

  HTML elements, 58

  K-nearest neighbors classifier, 57

  output console, 62

  predictClass method, 62

runPredictions function, 61

variable instantiation, 58

webcam input, 56

U, V

Unsupervised learning, 10–11

W, X, Y, Z

Word tokenization, 72

Printed in the United States
By Bookmasters